When I Was First Alone

a journey
from hurt to healing

Jan Johansen Stennes

LANGMARC PUBLISHING • **San Antonio, Texas**

When I Was First Alone
A Journey From Hurt to Healing

By Jan Johansen Stennes

Scripture taken from the HOLY BIBLE,
REVISED STANDARD VERSION
New Testament Section, © 1946; Old Testament Section, © 1952.
Thomas Nelson, Inc.

Editor: Renée Hermanson
Cover Art: Carolyn McBride
Text Illustrations: Cheryl Robey Overvig
Technical Layout: Michael Qualben

Published by LangMarc Publishing
Box 33817, San Antonio, TX 78265

Library of Congress Cataloging-in-Publication Data

Stennes, Jan Johansen
    When I was first alone : a journey from hurt to healing / by
Jan Johansen Stennes.
        p. cm.
    Includes index.
    ISBN 1-880292-08-4 (hardcover) : $12.95
    1. Divorce—Psychological aspects. I. Title.
HQ814.S79 1993   93-14794
306.89—dc20   CIP

In Memory of

My Brother

David Osmond Johansen

Dedication

To my children, Kristin, Karel, Kathryn, David, and their life partners, who expressed their love in countless ways when I needed it most.

To my parents, married 62 years at this writing, who reminded me of my strengths and encouraged me to strive for a new and better life.

To my precious friends, for bringing and sharing joy, laughter and tears; for their loving friendship, their strong example, and for their abundant love.

This book is also dedicated to all the men and women who have encountered loss through death, divorce, or broken relationships who are working to build a new and meaningful life.

⁓

An essential part of therapy is journaling. Although I didn't like the process, it proved to be therapeutic. Reviewing the entries years later proved that ground had been gained in the journey back to a meaningful life.

Looking back at the real feelings identified when I was first alone, I consider it necessary to tell everyone that there is hope—there is a way to find new life. I vowed then that if God helped me, I would help others recover from similar situations. I will keep my promise forever.

Foreword

There is such an avalanche of new books for the Christian community that one tends to wonder if we need one more. However, this is *not* a usual book. *When I Was First Alone: A Journey from Hurt to Healing* is a demonstration of how journal writing is not only a tool for self-knowledge, but a process for healing.

The writer indicates that, unless you are willing to take your spiritual life seriously, you'll never grow toward wholeness. Journaling helps you to do this. The creative process of a reflective journaling that led to writing this book helps one to see first hand God's creativity at work. Being creative is God working in us, but this energy can only be tapped when we release the things that block us—and Jan Stennes shows us first hand how this can happen. Through her journey toward healing, she shows that God is not absent or dull, but meets us at the growing edge of our lives.

To me, what is critical in a Christian book is whether or not it is biblical, whether it speaks from a personal experience and whether it has application. *When I Was First Alone* accomplishes all of the above. If you are separated, divorced, or widowed, this book will inspire and encourage you through your pain to know that healing is possible for you and that life can begin again.

Dr. Vernon J. Bittner, Director
Institute for Christian Living
Minneapolis, Minnesota
Author of—*Breaking Free,*
Twelve Steps to Christian Living,
You Can Help With Your Healing

Through Shadowed Valleys
1

Even though I walk through the
valley of the shadow of death...
thou art with me. Psalm 23:4

He is Gone

He is gone. He left last night. I must have been in shock, because I went to bed early and slept like a baby. I had attended an after-Christmas coffee gathering at his aunt's home and enjoyed visiting with women who are family and friends. He came for me late in the day. We drove home quietly.

On the way home, I basked in the glow of Christmas. I was tired, and I told him it would be good to be home this evening, to sit with him by candlelight and look at the tree lights, alone—together. It had been a busy week, with all the children and my parents with us for several days. Christmas at our house was steeped in tradition; it was a real celebration. I remember feeling so thankful, so complete. It felt good.

I hung my coat in the front closet. He went directly to the sofa, still wearing his coat. His face was gray and rigid. "Sit down," he said, "I want to talk with you." The tone of his voice was different. He was always so cheery. Something was very wrong. He told me he had been thinking, it had been a rough decision, but he was leaving, tonight, and would be making his January business trip to Texas earlier than originally planned. There was one exception. "I'm not coming back," he said, "and I'm going to get a divorce." There was a brief exchange of confused words which I cannot remember. He said he was leaving immediately; he was surprised I hadn't noticed all his clothes in the van as we drove home. I remember saying "Good-bye, Grampa!" at the door. Surely that would make him crumble! But he walked away and didn't look back. He was gone, forever. It was December 26, the day after Christmas. Our 29th wedding anniversary was to come on March 1.

I called my son and told him Dad had left! He was prepared for my call; his father told him the news earlier that day. He said, "Mom, I'll be right there." I went to his closet and found it empty, cleared of everything but a few hangers. I don't remember time passing, but soon David and Denise were embracing me tightly. We sobbed in each other's arms. Everything else is a blur. I called the girls and must have told them what happened. I don't remember. David stayed with me that night and prepared to move back home to watch over me.

The first months I was alone were the toughest I have ever faced. I lived in disbelief, anger, frustration and fear. I was physically and emotionally beaten. I lost 30 pounds off a frame that could not afford to lose more than 10. I slept as much as possible and disconnected with the outside world. Shame and guilt overcame me. I felt life was not worth living. But I had to continue because of my family, especially my parents. It was hell on earth.

Who Will Help Me?

Two days after he left, I telephoned my pastor. It was early afternoon, after he had returned home from Sunday services.

The sound of his voice, so warm and concerned, made me cry. He told me he had received a call from my husband the evening before. Hearing those words made it seem more final. He *must* be serious; he must not plan to come back! I was nearly crazy. I couldn't even talk to my husband. He would allow no discussion, and he was driving to an unknown destination.

"What am I going to do?" There was nothing in my stomach, but I wanted to throw up. Every nerve in my body was tingling. Was I going crazy? Is this how it feels when a person falls apart or has a total breakdown? I was so afraid. So afraid that I didn't dare tell my children how I felt inside. They'd be coming soon to check on me. David would be moving home today and Denise, his fiancée, would be spending most of her time with us. They were so upset, I couldn't frighten them even more. Perhaps they'd have to commit me! Where would I go? As I envisioned myself in a hospital room, drugged, I became nearly panic stricken. No treatment could help this. They'd want me to work on being alone and I didn't want to be alone! I just wanted him to come home, to hold me tightly and tell me it was a mistake. I wanted to call my parents, but what could they do? I'd frighten them so. They were 78 years old! I'd have to lose my mind on my own turf and someone would have to pick up the pieces. I didn't know who it would be. I just hoped *someone* would find me if something happened to me. My pastor suggested I seek counseling immediately but warned me to use care in my selection. The inability to communicate with my husband was smothering me. It seemed my life was being taken from me, and I could provide no defense!

As the day wore on and I wondered what to do, I thought about the church. After all, it *was* Sunday. We always attended worship services. Today I needed the church. Had he died, my living room wouldn't be empty. I'd have a pastoral call, without making an invitation. The neighbors would be coming and going and I wouldn't be alone to face reality. Here I was; alone, afraid, physically ill, and emotionally drained. Did the church have no capacity to reach out? I know it wasn't just my church—it was *any* church. Separation and divorce flew in the face of family concepts. Even if society was changing faster than the church, couldn't they help me?

The hideous feelings I endured the first days were magnified by my inability to communicate with my husband. He traveled the first several weeks and was out of contact with everyone except for occasional telephone calls to the children. After he settled in one location, he communicated once by letter and indicated he was thinking of returning. Then, he moved on and established himself for several months in another area of the country. So, with no contact or means of open communication, my grief displayed itself in a manner similar to those who endure the death of a spouse.

Combined with the horrible sense of loss was the fear of the future. My dreams had been shattered. I was exhausted and confused. I needed help and didn't know how to reach out. I was in a state of emotional paralysis.

I admire the congregations who have adopted the concept of hands-on, one-to-one involvement with people in need. There are times, even to someone as self-sufficient as I appeared, when caring support is vital to mental health. I needed to have a caring friend at my side to remind me I was still God's precious child—not a cast-off wife.

David

I wish you were here. You'd be the only one I could talk to in the whole world. As brother and sister, we shared everything. You knew how I felt before I knew. I knew you just as well. We protected each other.

I need you now to hold me up, to help me know that I'll be fine some day. You could be strong for me. They say I'll be strong some day. Today I'm not. You wouldn't know me today, Dave. I'm beaten.

I know you're in Heaven. Will you ask God to pay special attention to me? And somehow, somehow will you hang on to me? I need you.

§

My brother David passed away when I was 26 and he was 24. We were like twins. When he died of a rare disease, a piece of me died with him.

Now I cherish his memory and wish he were here, as I always do, to hold my hand, to love and enjoy my children, to enhance my life with his contagious laughter and warmth.

We hold dear the memories of those we loved so intensely. We want to be strong, as they would want us to be strong. We need to honor their faith in us.

David would want me to be strong.

The Ghosts of Christmases Past

I went "home" to my parents' home a few days after he left. I couldn't stand to be alone, so on New Year's Eve I offered to care for my grandchildren, who lived in the same town.

Returning to my own home a few days later, to the remnants of that last Christmas together, was a jolt. I put my things in the bedroom and immediately began to remove the trimmings from the tree and the house. Our home was always decorated from end to end. We loved the holiday season, entertained many guests, and thoroughly enjoyed our "Christmas house."

I'll never forget that day. I felt like throwing everything in the garbage, but I reminisced at each item I touched. The silver bell marked with the words "25 Wonderful Years Together" moved me to convulsive sobs.

I recalled Christmases when the children were little; happy times. I remembered friends gathering at our home for candlelight dinners. We had so much fun, and those special times were indeed so special! The angel at the top of the tree was purchased when Kris was a baby. It had enhanced each Christmas through the years. How could I ever have another Merry Christmas?

Since that time, Christmas has never returned without the memory of that fateful "day after." It becomes less difficult each year, due to the passage of time and my efforts to create new experiences. I must admit, however, that it is a relief to remove the trimmings and return to "normal" after the holiday season.

Our Bedroom

It was finished the week before Christmas. We had often admired the cozy bedroom on the Bob Newhart television show; everything matched, with lots of pillows. We wanted a room just like it.

I found bedding in a paisley pattern of subtle blues and mauves. While visiting a country shop, I had noticed the various styles of curtains but especially admired those done in "bishops sleeves." I also liked the balloon valances. I purchased lace panels and bought sheets to convert into valances and sleeves. Then I made a comforter for our king-size bed. I covered lots of pillows with the same pattern and converted our room into something from a designer's showcase. It was nifty! It was ready for Christmas, so our guests used the room during the holiday week. We didn't get to use it—not even once.

After several weeks I took down the curtains that reminded me of "our" room. I was proud of them because I made them without a pattern. The room was still beautiful, but it had become only a place to sleep and was no longer a comfortable haven.

Some day I'll redo that room. Then it will be mine. The paper will be subtle. It will take on a Scandinavian country theme, like the rest of my home. It will be comfortable and mine, just mine.

Sleep

Sleep was taken for granted. He slept on the side closest to the doorway. That's where he always slept, as if to protect me from harm. At least that's how I felt.

I moved over to his side of the bed after he left, hoping to sleep. The fragrance of his cologne remained in his pillow for weeks. I'd awaken many times, hoping I had heard the welcome sounds of his return. I didn't hear those sounds, though I longed for them for several months.

It was nearly impossible to relax. My electric blanket was turned up to the highest temperature, the radio on low playing hours of talk-radio. I was exhausted and didn't want to be exposed to the outside world. So I retreated to my lonely bed in early evening, attempting to find comfort and security, hiding from everything and everyone. It was difficult to stretch into my full length; the fetal position was natural for me now. At times my body ached from tension. I longed for his touch, to hear him snore. I'd awaken, waiting for him to turn over and throw his arm over me. Then I'd remember.

Months passed, months of fitful sleep. Then one morning I awakened to find myself sprawled out in the middle of the bed, in peace. I sat up in disbelief, startled at this discovery, and exclaimed out loud to myself, "Thank you, God!" I had finally conquered this place!

The doctor said I don't require so much sleep. Perhaps that is true. He prescribed relaxants at first, when I asked for them, and they made the nights comfortable. But I'd still awaken often with tension in my body. On one visit, he told me he should prescribe no more. I panicked. How would I ever sleep? But I did. My

mind had gradually relaxed; the situation was becoming tolerable and rest was achieved.

I've learned to relax. I try to eliminate caffeine after dinner (that includes chocolate!) and to read after an evening of excited conversation. I'll watch television late at night, often falling asleep on the sofa. Sleep comes soon, and it's good.

Dreams

Someone said dreams are the wishes of the conscious mind. One night I dreamed I awakened to see him in the hallway, standing in the doorway in his coat, smiling, and saying, "You awake?" I was so happy. I believed I saw him in the doorway—believed I had dreamed his absence. Lo, it had all been a bad dream! I heaved a huge sigh and sat up in bed. Then I awakened and heard nothing, saw nothing. *This* was real. This was hell!

Nothing is so cruel as a dream when it comes as the good fairy, bringing you the utmost desires of your heart, and leaves you as a thief in the night. So many dreams recalled his pattern of arriving home late at night after a meeting. The sounds of the garage door opening, the squeak of the door knob in the living room, the snap of the light switch in the hallway, were real. They brought moments of bliss, followed by the crash of despair. To call his name in the night, certain he'd answer, yet afraid he would not, left me so vulnerable— so afraid.

The Neighbors

How could I tell them? Those whom we love so dearly. We often sat outside together on nice evenings, always laughing and joking together. They are all fine people. They like us as much as we like them. They'll think we're crazy!

Because my husband was away on short trips quite often, they noticed he was gone but never knew if he had returned and left on another trip. I walked through the snow one dark winter night and rang the doorbell, trembling with emotion. Bonnie and Clay asked me to come in and sit down. The warmth of their home and the sight of the two of them together, with me alone, overcame me. I began to cry and said, "He's gone, he wants a divorce and he's not coming back." Bonnie held me in her arms as I sat next to her, while Clay hung his head in dismay. I had given them a terribly heavy load to bear. Clay facilitated the Twelve Steps for Christian Living group at church, and he encouraged my participation whenever I felt I was ready.

Dorothy and Lee had to be told right away. I knew the news would devastate them. Even though we were such close friends, I couldn't face her. I hoped she hadn't noticed he was gone. I finally worked up the courage to tell her—over the telephone. That evening, as I walked out onto the deck for a breath of fresh winter air, Lee came out of his garage, looked over at me and said, "Hi, Jan" in a low, sad voice, and walked toward me. We cried together as we held each other. Lee said, "I just don't understand him. He had everything here."

I felt much more protected, knowing these people now shared my grief and concern. The men discussed home safety with me, urging me to order a yard light.

They provided me with decals for my doors and windows indicating I was electronically protected. They invited me for coffee, out for dinner, and to concerts. It didn't feel good to be the odd person, but they were so considerate and sensitive I could only be thankful. They made me feel like their younger sister.

We've returned to normal, enjoying our friendship and fun as neighbors. (They're even suggesting names of potential suitors!)

God placed me where He knew I'd be loved and cared for, long before I knew what lay in store for me!

Abandoned

I'm all alone. I don't know what to do. Patty was here for the weekend. It was always so much fun when she came to visit, but this time it seemed strange. I'm so horribly preoccupied.

I tried to prepare food and I didn't know how! I've forgotten! Patty always said I taught her everything she knows about entertaining and creating wonderful food. She does such a lovely job of hosting. So did I, at one time. This weekend, I didn't know what to do first! I used to be able to prepare many things at a time, juggling all the preparations and finishing two hours ahead so I could get ready for guests—and then relax. Now I'd have to work three days, carefully preparing, for one dinner party. This is craziness. What's going on with my mind?

I couldn't laugh. We didn't have fun. And then it was time for her to leave. I burst into tears the moment the door was closed behind her. I wanted her to stay, but she couldn't. If I were her, I wouldn't stay either.

I felt abandoned. She must have wondered what else is wrong...what's *really* wrong here? It's more than him leaving. It's just that I feel so alone and I don't know how to handle it. When someone comes who was so much a part of "us," it's like they enter this place as if it's another world. I hate it. I hate this life.

I fought the feeling of abandonment for months. Because of the darkness of winter, perhaps, and the darkness of my spirit, I felt like I was someone else. I didn't know who I was any longer, and I just wanted someone to move in and take care of me.

As the seasons changed, my spirit changed as well. Spring brought open doors and windows and a feeling of connection with the world, with nature. I "connect" with nature in touching a leaf, in planting seeds. I walked in the park and joined in the spirit of growth around me.

At times I felt like the "motherless child" the old song records. As confidence returned, I was able to connect again with the world—with people. But, looking back, I'm convinced abandonment is the worst feeling there is.

What Can They Say?

Here I am, alone. How can I see anyone? Some are so kind, so loving; but what are they really thinking? Do they wonder what's *really* wrong with me? What's the *real* reason he left?

I see them looking at me. I "feel" others looking at me. I'm grossly paranoid. If only they knew how I hurt. I feel set apart. I'm like a freak. I am different and will never be like the others again. My life must be over.

I want to be with them, the others, but one at a time. I can't possibly be with a group of people, not even a few. I want them to talk with me, to talk about me—in my presence. If the conversation moves away from me into normal household prattle, I won't be able to stand it. I don't have that stuff to talk about anymore. I can't think about what I'm going to make us for dinner because he's not here anymore. I can't think of plans for the weekend, of anything in the future. There is no more future. It's gone. They don't understand. They have no idea.

I'm afraid someone will tell me it's going to be all right. It will never be all right. What is going to happen?

I try to remember how I felt then. I try to remember the exact feelings. I do remember, and I still feel the pain and emptiness. It's an awful feeling. But it's different now. I never thought it would be, but it is. It's different.

I must remember, most importantly, simply to be there if I know someone in a similar situation. It isn't important to come with news, with prattle to take their mind off the subject at hand. It doesn't work. It just sets it aside—and we're not heard anyway.

It's good to go elsewhere—preferably someplace that doesn't hold memories—to talk. A change of scenery—a walk in a different area—just for a little while—felt so good. Fresh air and sunlight were the lifeblood of each day. I was first alone in the darkness of winter. It was horrible.

The best medicine friends can give is to listen, and listen, and listen, and listen.

We are "tried" as friends when we minister to a hurting friend. I remember feeling that I belabored some friends with the same subject. I had so much to say, and I had to say it over and over and over. They listened. They listened for hours at a time. Day after day, they listened.

And when the day came that recovery was on the horizon, they were overjoyed. Their joy was sincere.

It is in times of trouble that we show our love. We know that love changes everything.

Longing

Longing must be the feeling of being almost desperate. It happens when you ache to be held, when you fear no one will ever hold you again. Sometimes longing hurts with tremendous pain. Longing is tricky. Sometimes I long to be with the kids. When I'm with them, I long to be home alone. Then I don't have to "pretend." Longing is such a strong desire. I just wish I knew what I was longing for. I long to be held, to snuggle! I guess I just long to be like I was before all this happened.

I don't "long" much any more. There are times, though, when I wish there was someone to hold me. Not just one of the kids, but someone who would stand there and hold me and talk softly to me while I melted. Or, in the morning, after I turn up the heat and return to my bed while the house warms. It was a favorite time to snuggle—but difficult to get up! It was wonderful.

Touch deprivation causes real pain, as recognized in therapy today. A hug, an arm around a shoulder, a hand clasp—all are designed to bring comfort and security to the human being.

Pain

Emotional pain hurts! I couldn't believe it. The pain would rise in my chest and my entire body ached. It was much worse in a group situation, and nearly unbearable in familiar settings or with old friends. As time passed, the second time at any event or in any circumstance was less painful. Gradually, these occasions became pain free.

I never understood why people referred to the "pain of heartbreak." How could emotions "hurt"? But pain set in and wouldn't leave. I'd walk into my home after work and leave the lights off. I ached so badly, all over my body. I longed to be touched, to be held, to know that someone cared. I would sit in the dark and wonder what life held for me. Obviously, nothing. The pain worsened.

There is no more pain. It lasted nearly two years, but it left me one day. It recurs rarely; it's most likely to return on a lovely summer evening when I'm home alone, sitting outside on the deck—wishing I weren't alone.

Church

This haven, this place of rest and hope. This place where I should go to feel renewed. Several weeks passed before I could return to church, and it was one of the most difficult things I have ever done. As a couple, we took great joy from our church. We loved music and enjoyed our fine organ and choir. We were inspired by every sermon and other parts of the worship service. We were truly fed, together, by this experience.

But this was awful! I knew I'd cry and might not be able to stop. I didn't dare sit in a pew filled with people, so I sat in the balcony in the place we sat together (he ushered in that section). Then I felt people were looking at me. Why would they? Our congregation is very large and I wasn't well known. It was just me. I was so ashamed, so overcome with grief. Here, in God's house, I was no longer a "whole" person. I felt like a half person with a husband who didn't want me. I couldn't accept that. I knew God loved me, no matter what. But I didn't love me, and I was ashamed. After all, my husband had left me.

Afterwards I went home, alone. Is there anything worse than being alone on Sunday? I always prepared a huge Sunday dinner when he was home with me. I was proud of my old-fashioned habits. Why does everything have to be so miserable? Oh my God, why?

Eventually it became obvious I could no longer sit where we sat together for many years, so I simply moved downstairs to the section below, closer to the front. I could see the altar and the pastors clearly. I was alone there, which felt good. Today I don't mind being alone in church. Friends often gather for a chat and coffee in the lounge before leaving for home. It's a good day to gather

*family or friends for brunch and visit for half the after-noon. One day (I hope) someone will be with me again—to enjoy the worship—together. Now I don't **feel** alone. I feel the presence of God, and it's comforting and wonderful.*

I Can't Read!

It shocked me! I picked up the newspaper and took my seat on the sofa in the living room where we always had Sunday morning coffee. It would now be my special place, every day, for coffee and the morning paper. But, somehow I couldn't read! I had to concentrate so heavily, and the meaning of the words escaped me. I looked at the pictures and could assume their meaning. This began a long period of "looking at the paper," a time of making lists and exerting a great effort concerning anything in printed form. I was planning to return to full-time work. How could I? The appointment with my doctor was coming in a few days. Should I tell him? It frightened me. What if I had something very wrong with me?

My doctor must be the kindest physician there is. When I worked up the courage to tell him my problem, he very patiently explained that my brain was over-burdened. "The red light is on, Jan! You're on over-load!"

Then he gave me some very good advice. He stressed the importance of a balanced life. He asked me what kind of exercise I did, reviewed my diet and questioned my sleep patterns.

Then he asked, "Are you having fun?" I had to think a moment. "Fun?" I thought. I remembered fun, but it was no longer part of my life. What a shame. I had always liked to have fun—people said I was a fun person. How could I have fun in this situation? Besides, who would I have fun with?

The Work Place

I don't want to go back to work to face the people who thought my marriage was the perfect one. They'll think I failed "big time." I will be embarrassed and humiliated.

Vicki gave unselfishly of her time to listen and to share her experiences. She explained how to re-enter the social scene, told me of various singles organizations, warned me about the men who wander from one group to another looking for the "new woman" and never seem to improve their emotional state. It seems to be a sad scenario.

Soon I'll be divorced and I'll be one of them. I hate the trappings of this new status. Vicki suggested it was time for me to join her in this new world of single people. All I knew was that I didn't like being classified—the term "divorce" isn't one I will carry easily. It sounds so cheap, and I refuse to be classified as cheap.

But I must admit, I've been keeping my eyes open. There's no one out there for me. And I'm not interested in replacing him, not yet.

After a great deal of healing took place and my self-respect returned, it became apparent the secular scene was not going to be for me. Why should I even consider it? I could not. It was at this time that I withdrew into my inner self, where I found solace.

I was learning to live in solitude. A new foundation was being prepared for this new era of my life.

My Children

Bless them, each of my children. They are God's gift to me, His message to me that I did something very right in my life.

All four of them, with their partners, watched me for months, many months. They listened to me, they held me as I cried, all so very patiently and lovingly. And when they had heard enough, when time had passed, they all said, "Enough, Mom, enough."

I'd cry before they came home to visit, and I'd cry after they left. It was so good to have them with me, and so quiet when they left. Life was changing before my eyes, and I could do nothing to rescue myself. Our family had been forced into drastic change.

I felt sorry for them; my God, how sorry I was. They loved their father so much. He represented fun and happiness; then he turned and left. What must they feel? They longed for him as much as I did. Their concerns were for our well-being, together and separately. If one parent is peaceful and the other unsettled, it disturbs them. We were all so helpless, but why them? Every mother does all she can to protect her children. I could do nothing and I knew my pain was hurting them even more.

When I got back to good health and looked as if I'd make it, they'd see me dressed for an event and would remark, "Mom! You look great!" Of all the people in this world, no one deserved to see me look good again more than these children of mine who suffered the agony with me. They are so responsible, so caring.

Divorce breaks children's hearts, no matter what their age. Just because they're married and living else-where does not lessen their hurt. They expect Mom and

Dad to be there for them, together. We had been very young parents, always responsive to our kids and their needs. They returned our love and respect.

I am very proud of these loving, responsible children.

Romans 8:28

Kris, my eldest daughter, wears her heart on her sleeve, just like her mother. Her eyes are very brown and very large. She'd look at me, at times, with wider eyes, and I knew how she was feeling. She watched me without saying a word. I felt I knew what she was thinking because our thought processes always have been similar. It was easier for her to select a card or write a lovely note than to say the words directly to me, which would have brought uncontrollable tears. I loved receiving her cards of support. There were many; they came often.

One of the most poignant cards I received during the first months was a lovely card illustrated with a sweet-faced angel sitting on a cloud. Inside; was the Bible verse as recorded in Romans, the eighth chapter, the 28th verse. "We know that in everything God works for good with those who love him, who are called according to his purpose." [RSV] Beneath the verse was her hand-written message, "If there's anything I can do..." How thrilling to know one of my children was sharing Scripture with me as my hope. That verse became a leaning post through the ensuing months. There had to be a reason—some good would have to come of this.

Stress

It's so hard to breathe! There are times when I realize my breathing is very shallow. Then I take a deep breath or two and nearly cave in from exhaustion. I have to be careful about breathing—I'm afraid I will hyperventilate. I know it's from stress. It must be. Sometimes a feeling of anxiety nearly overcomes me. I try to think—to remember—is something else going on? Why does this awful feeling come over me at times?

My doctor was gentle but firm about my cholesterol count. I could hardly believe the count could elevate 100 points just from stress. I'd guess if the rest of me clogs up and nearly shuts down, my arteries may as well join in. Fat intake is dangerous, I know, but I'm hardly eating anything.

I have to remember to eat properly, too. I can hardly eat at all. Ish! It doesn't even feel good to write those words. And exercise? I just don't have the energy. I recall, though, the night Shirley and I walked in a snowstorm to a grocery store. As we walked up the driveway to the house, I was surprised that my sadness wasn't there—until I opened the door. The walk was one mile round trip. So I know exercise is a stress reliever.

I don't have trouble sleeping, but I have trouble sleeping for a very long time. Three hours in one "sleep" is a big deal. I'm tired, though, and need to go to bed early to allow for this gap in the middle of the night.

My friend Joni reminds me to think good thoughts, to write positive affirmations on paper and place them where they'll be seen and repeated. Somehow I've got to keep stress at a minimum. If anything else happens, I could be in real trouble.

Diet, exercise and rest are so very important. I have always taken a quality multi-vitamin every day.

Breakfast was not easy to eat, but I forced myself to have one slice of toast while getting ready to go to work in the morning. The days I was home, it was easier to wait an hour to eat more substantially.

Unlike many people, my throat seems to close when I'm stressed. People who have weight problems envy this, but stress could starve me if I didn't realize how dangerous it could be.

Beside Still Waters
2

...He leadeth me beside still waters;
He restoreth my soul. Psalm 23:2

Therapy

I hated therapy at first. I met privately with a therapist for several sessions. He suggested I join a women's group to identify many of the issues I would face. We met, eight of us, in a comfortable, large office with two sofas, lots of soft pillows (to pound in our anger!) and soft lighting. It was like being at home, but it was very painful. Each of us had a chance to tell her story, while the other seven women sat and listened in amazement. It didn't take very long for me to realize I was the most fortunate participant. I had never been beaten or treated poorly. One young woman had so many problems, it seemed she would never overcome them. Why did she stay with a husband who was so disrespectful? Didn't she respect herself at all? And my contemporary, so pretty and intelligent, crying because her husband would not give up his girlfriend. I wondered why I needed to be there. They were the ones who needed help.

But I learned that we had different needs for help. Each of us found reasons for unhappiness planted deep within our lives. It was necessary to dredge the "garbage" from our past lives, to deal with the present and work on growth.

Thankfully, there are talented Christian counselors in our city. It was good to be able to counsel with people who hold the same values, who want only to help in a healing process.

We met weekly. Soon I was anxious for Thursday, when I would see these new friends and learn more about myself. Then, one evening, I was making excuses for my husband's sudden departure, stating I was certain he'd be home soon, convinced he'd send me money as soon as he had extra cash, covering for him totally. One of my group members said, "Get it through your head, Jan. He left *you*. He isn't worrying about *you*. He's probably spending his money on someone else and here you are, defending him!" I became angry, then burst into tears. I had always defended him, but she was right on target. I couldn't bear to hear her words. I was an enabler! I was protecting him at my own expense! How I cried! The dam had burst in my heart and soul. Now I was ready for the healing process to begin.

Therapy is absolutely necessary. It was difficult because I have always been a private person. I had never shared my feelings with anyone before. But there was no other way to begin my quest for healing and peace. I had to first dredge up the pain and wallow in it for a time, and become ill from it. Every day from the moment of that discovery has become a step on the road back to sanity and peace.

Therapy is costly. My insurance plan did not cover the costs, but I felt it was a necessity and sacrificed to afford it.

I have learned things about myself and, even more importantly—about others—that make me more understanding. When I hear someone "confess" they have been in therapy, I admire them greatly. I know the courage it takes and the pain they have suffered in their effort to reach a place of peace. Thank God we live in this era of personal growth through healing therapy!

Familiar Scenes

The rains persisted for a week that first spring. My pain persisted like the rain. I so vividly recall sitting with Nancy in a restaurant in my office building. Through the windows, I saw trees on the boulevard, black against the dismal skies. It was a bleak scene as I sat there listening to Nancy's part of our conversation and trying to concentrate on her words. That day I couldn't talk with her about my feelings. She didn't know how badly I hurt, nor could she feel the longing in my heart. I was mesmerized by the dismal scene that matched my mood.

Such occasions happened often. Nearly everything I did the first year I was alone was done with similar feelings of agony. I wanted to be home, to be alone even more.

One day I walked into that same restaurant, made my selection from the trays of morning coffee treats, and proceeded towards the cashier who was busily making change for the people ahead of me. As I waited, I glanced toward the window and my heart seemed to drop in my chest. Then I remembered. It's okay, you're okay now. The scene was the very same as that day, a few years ago. But today there is a difference. Today I'm so happy, so very happy. Life isn't perfect, but will it ever be truly perfect?

One thing is certain…today is different from that day I sat there and looked at the trees on the boulevard. Today I know those trees will bud and leaf out, nurtured by the rains. Thank God! This new life is a victory.

Couples

Couples make me sick. They're everywhere! I hadn't noticed this before. It seems that wherever I go, whatever I do, I am aware of the numerous couples in the world.

I am most irritated on the weekends by couples who are all dressed up as they drive by in their freshly cleaned cars—obviously going someplace special. I'd turn my lights off and sit in the dark, wishing I weren't there.

I see older couples, helping each other so carefully. They treat each other tenderly, lovingly.

My kids are couples, my parents are a couple, most of my friends are couples. I was part of a couple. It was comfortable. I felt protected. Now I'm alone.

℘

Two years passed before I could tolerate "couples" in society. Now, I can be in their company and feel fortunate to be "me." Don't get me wrong. I'd love to be part of a couple! But God hasn't found anyone for me yet. I don't know if there is someone in "the wings" who would meet my long and strict list of qualifications. Meanwhile, I enjoy my married friends and love to be with them.

Summer

What is this curse called Summer? I have six weeks available for vacations each year. What on earth can I do alone?

Here I am. Others are thinking of slowing their pace, starting to enjoy this good time of life. My neighbors pack their cars each weekend for trips to their lake cabins. I could be doing that. I've always wanted a cabin and now, certainly, that hope is lost. Nothing is fun when you're alone.

Everyone is gone. Again I ask God, "What did I do? Can't you just tell me somehow? Can't *you* forgive whatever it was? Who are you anyway? This is mean. It's just plain mean to do this to me in the prime of my life!" What could be so bad as to be imprisoned in my own home? This time of year is now a curse called Summer, when organized society takes a break to enjoy life.

I loved this time of beauty, when flowers begin to bloom, the sun rises early so I can walk and enjoy a breath of nature. I fill my coffee cup and walk around the yard in my robe early in the morning, sipping in the delicious sights and smells together with my morning refreshment.

Alone. I detest the word, the condition. Summer means alone.

The Fourth of July, ironically, was the worst of all days to endure. Since I was a child, it had been a festive day of parades, picnics and people. This was another day of traditions. For decades, our family had spent the Fourth with the Osens and other family friends.

In my neighborhood it doesn't seem very festive; all the neighbors are at their summer cabins. As I sit on the deck, I wonder what I've done to deserve this isolation. The festivities were often at my house, and now the deck was bathed in deafening sounds of silence. The children were off with friends having their own festivities. They had spent every holiday with me during the year, so this day must have been a "break" for them, away from the heaviness of thoughts of what had been.

Summers are long. It seems they're filled with little stuff, nothing special; just little stuff to turn the weekends into something useful or meaningful. I hate it...I just hate it! Yes, I can drive 130 miles to visit my parents, but even *they* are together there. My friends in that town are at their cabins, too, or doing something fun together on these lovely summer weekends. Everyone I know is married. I don't fit anywhere.

I love to garden and watch nature produce its finest. Summer is the only time this happens in Minnesota. I must spend more weekends away. I must invite people to my home more often. Summer festivals, concerts in the parks, long walks, all can help me enjoy the beauty of summer. New projects will require concentration. Summer will go fast—too fast! It would be fun to have a boy friend.

Even as the years passed, I've been haunted with memories on the Fourth of July. Summer holidays can be difficult. I don't want to create an event to replace old memories; I have to make new ones. We can always gather for a picnic. Perhaps we'll go to see the fireworks display. Whatever I do, it won't replace the fun we used to have on the Fourth of July. Life changes and gets better, with effort. There has to be one glitch, I'd guess, and this is it!

Going to the Well

I visited my parents every two weeks the first several months I was alone. I needed the assurance that they were enduring this terrible time, and they needed to see that I was making slow progress. Kris and Mike and their children lived next to them, so my visits were pleasant times. The little children loved it when I came, and I was provided with all the hugs and kisses I needed.

One summer weekend the youngsters were gone, so I was alone with my parents. It seemed particularly lonesome. I felt like a little girl as I saw the pity in their faces. This has been so difficult for them, and it killed me to think my life had made them miserable.

It was a hot and humid Saturday. Suddenly the emotions of the day and my aloneness overcame me like an unquenchable thirst. I got into my car to go for a ride, not knowing where I'd go. I seemed to be in a time warp. We had been part of the "fun" crowd, always going places and doing things. Now I was alone and nearly beaten.

I drove past the church. We had worked so hard on that building project and took such pride in what had been accomplished. So much of our lives revolved around this very church. I wondered if anyone was there—if it was open. It was! I always felt better when I was inside the church.

As I entered the narthex, I could hear someone talking on the telephone in the office down the hallway. The pastor was there. As I stood in the doorway, he acknowledged my presence and pointed to a chair. He finished his telephone conversation and asked, "Are you all right?" I wanted to cry, to burst. I told him of my desperate feelings of aloneness. He gave me words of wisdom and Scripture that allowed me to find temporary peace. I thanked him and left, grateful that I could find cooling, healing words there, in my home church, with my parents' pastor. At worship services the next morning, the sermon spoke to my concerns. Afterwards Mother said, "Did you feel he was speaking to you?" "Yes," I said, "he was."

Over the years I have been fortunate to hear many similar sermons at that church, each one carefully prepared to minister through the Gospel to the individual, hurting soul. I am always so enriched by this pastor's messages and know he is a special shepherd called to enlighten his people. Many times as I shake his hand at the door, I am glad to tell him, "Being here is like going to the well."

Dependency

I hate being labeled "dependent" or "co-dependent." When we live with someone for many years, we are naturally dependent on one another. I depended on you to bring home the paychecks, to take care of the service on the cars, to help with the yard work. You depended on me to keep our home clean and pleasant, to care for our clothes, to prepare meals, to be there for you, and on and on. We depend on others for goods and services. Why, then, is marriage dependency so different, so unusual?

I can live without you. I don't like it, but I can. It's just that I don't *want* to live without you. I want you in my life because I love you. It's that simple.

Remember the Cynthia Clawson tape we used to play when we were in the car together? We loved some of the songs and skipped over some that were unfamiliar. You took the tape with you when you left so I bought another one and play it often. One song talks about asking God to "heal this discontent in the Winter of my soul." My soul is in Winter right now. I suppose if God ever decides to heal it, it will find Summer again—or at least, perhaps, Spring.

My heart aches at the thought of being without you. I'm getting used to the idea, though. I'm learning how, bit by bit. I'm awfully lucky to have such good, caring therapy at the Institute for Christian Living. It's helping. It's really good for me. It will take time, but I'll manage some day. Just watch me.

Dr. Vern Bittner, in Breaking Free, *discusses dependency in his chapter entitled, "Little Hope Without the Believing":*

"I have discovered that when we give up our dependency needs to be consoled, understood, and loved, we die in a very real sense, and sometimes something new has a chance to live and grow within us. We begin to see that giving understanding and love is more important than receiving it. And if we continue in this way, we lose our unsatisfying lives and what we thought was important.... Our focus must be on Christ, for we are dependent on Him. This focus alone leads to health and wholeness. We die to the old fears and false securities, and are raised, filled with the hope which only Christ can give. We have been transformed, and weakness has been turned into strength, and fear has been replaced by hope. You see, there is LITTLE HOPE WITHOUT BELIEVING....'that a power who came in the person of Jesus Christ...can transform' our lives."

Breaking Free by Vernon J. Bittner
© 1986 Prince of Peace Publishing, Inc.
Burnsville, Minnesota

I knew early in this process that I could no longer depend on my estranged husband. It was a startling bit of knowledge, one that nearly devastated me. It was a disappointment of monumental consequence.

I knew then that there was only one upon whom I could lean, steadfastly. "Our focus must be on Christ... This focus alone leads to health and wholeness." Thank God for that knowledge. I knew I would, one day, find both health and wholeness.

You Can Do It, Sister

My brother, Tom, stopped by to spend a day. He had traveled from Tucson to spend a few days in northern Minnesota visiting our parents. I welcomed the hours we could spend together awaiting his late afternoon flight.

We sat outside on the deck. It was a difficult day in some ways. Previously, when an infrequent visitor like Tom spent time with us, other people were there as well. Today it was just me, alone with my younger brother, my friend.

We talked about the children. He asked important questions about my finances and generally checked on his sister to be sure everything was in place.

In our family, personal finance was never discussed. So Tom's open, loving question about money was surprising, but honest. He cared so much and was concerned that I could manage myself well.

After a time of discussion, of sharing my concerns, the horrors of the previous year and apprehensions for the future, he smiled as only my handsome brother can smile and said, "You'll make it through this, Jan. You're going to make it, and you're going to make it in such a big way you won't believe it yourself!"

"Oh Tommy," I said, "I don't need to make it in a big way. I just need to make it."

Tom's words of encouragement were so welcome. He spoke in a tone of absolute positiveness. There was no room for doubt in our conversation. I was going to make it because my brother said I would! He wanted me to!

It's wonderful to have a brother to lean on, even if he's far away. It's wonderful to receive a quick telephone

43

call, to answer the phone saying, "Hi, Tom, what's up?" and to hear a warm, "Nothing. Just calling to tell you I love you and ask what's new! And how are Mom and Dad?"

Safety

Someone broke into the neighbors' house last evening. Dorothy was downstairs and heard someone at the back door. Monday was Lee's bowling night. He wasn't expected home for nearly an hour. Their dog charged up the stairs and stopped frozen on the stairway. The robber had quietly taken the back door off, bolts and all, to take Dorothy's purse from the kitchen table. That's all I need, another kind of fear! Maybe I should just consider moving back up north. Half the people there don't bother to lock their doors at all! This is getting crazy. There have been several robberies in our neighborhood, just a block away. We live in a lovely area and don't anticipate such problems.

The robbery, although relatively minor, became a major event in my life as it related to my own safety. My home security system was installed, but a policeman friend of the family suggested that a talented robber would know how to foil the system. He said noise and light are the major deterrents.

I brought out a few pairs of David's shoes and arranged them to appear that he had kicked them off in front of each door every evening. My purse was hidden from view. I often turned on the radio if I left the house for the evening, and turned on a few more lights. I don't know that my measures foiled any burglary attempts, but it made me feel more secure.

The Search for "Me"

Today I spent hours thinking about Me. Who am I? It's Sunday, a bright and sunny Sunday in the fall. I've been alone all day, working in the yard and in my "secret garden" at the edge of my front yard. It's a lovely spot bordering my neighbor's yard. Pine trees shade the garden most of the day, so it is planted with hosta and dramatic rose begonias, with the brilliant colors of dianthus at the border. Clay, my neighbor, lined the pathway through the garden with wood chips as he said, "There will always be a path to 'our' house." It gave me a sense of community in my solitude.

So what does life hold for me? Will I always retreat to my secret garden for peace? And when it rains, and when winter returns, will I still long for my secret garden for my *only* sense of peace?

"Who," I wondered, "were you before all of this happened?" It was difficult to remember at first. I sat on my front steps, soaking up the afternoon sun. It was very quiet, except for the mourning doves which seemed to haunt me with their sad and somber song.

And I remembered: Activity, busyness, my calendar on the wall, filled with jottings reminding me of commitments and opportunities. I remembered people surrounding me. I remembered being available for others in their times of trouble and being a giving person. Now I was on the receiving end and could not summon the strength to reach out.

More memories flooded in: Music and the huge part it played in my life; projects, sewing for the girls and myself and knitting for all of us, painting and decorating my home, anticipating the arrival of the "Better Homes and Gardens" each month for new ideas, new recipes. I remembered working in the flower beds before the others were awake each morning. I remembered baking something every day, of being excited about preparing a special dinner each evening. I remembered entertaining guests, loving to plan events and using every opportunity to fill our large home with special people, and feeling life was wonderful and full.

All these memories remind me that I once had ambition and vitality. Where did it go? Would I ever—ever—regain even a part of it? The memories of days gone by made me smile to myself. That life was so happy. No one could give it back to me. It was up to me. Only I could start over and reclaim the life I had once enjoyed so much. Somehow I would do it. Sitting there, as the sun moved to the west and shaded my porch, I knew that too many days would move as quickly as this one. I would not—I could not—waste many more days dreaming of the days gone by.

The search for "Me" was conducted in quiet times. The periods when I ran away—working at the office all day and getting involved in activities each evening and weekend—only delayed the search.

I needed to be alone at times, to reflect on the person who had lived such a full life, and to decide how to reclaim that life. The gradual blending of other activities helped me rebuild and move ahead.

The effort was worth it. Now I have flowers, music, patterns, people, projects—and I have a new subscription to "Better Homes and Gardens"!

Lisa

My financial obligations were monumental. We had purchased our home on the basis of two incomes. Now with only me working half time, changes had to be made. The entire lower level of my home was vacant. It was designed as a mother-in-law apartment, which made it a great place for the children in their teen years. I decided to rent out the apartment.

Lisa was referred by a friend. The referral may have come from Janet, but Lisa was sent by God. We liked each other immediately. She loved the apartment and said she'd move in the following week.

Lisa played the viola in the symphony. She created a music studio in the room below mine. I loved to lie on my bed in the early evening, listening to the pure strains of her beautiful music. Lisa became synonymous with peacefulness.

One spring day, as we sat outside on the deck drinking our strong, Norwegian coffee, she lamented that she "hadn't been taking enough quiet time with the Lord." I was amazed that this young woman was serious! I asked her about this quiet time, and she told me how she read the Scriptures, prayed, and then quietly "listened" for God's input each day. I felt ashamed that I hadn't tapped this power source, readily available through the Holy Spirit. I knew that! Where had I been? I was so busy thinking about myself and what came next that I hadn't remembered what I knew so well. "Ask, and it shall be given you; seek, and ye shall find; knock, and it shall be opened unto you." (Matthew 7:7)

Along with the gift of Lisa came the gift of Anne Marie and George. Lisa's parents were my age, and we immediately became fast friends. Two years later George

died of cancer. I had never known such a crusader for Christ, a man who shared his faith so openly. It's no wonder Lisa is such a strong Christian.

Anne Marie and I were now in the same situation and our friendship has been a blessing to both of us. I will always have a place in her home in Tucson, and she in mine. We love the same things, we are both pure Norwegian, and we feel as comfortable in concert dress as in hiking boots!

The two years Lisa lived in my home saw many changes in my life. Lisa's friendship was a stepping stone into this most important part of my healing.

Twelve Steps to Healing

My neighbor is the facilitator of a Monday evening group at my church entitled, "Twelve Steps for Christian Living." We met there to review the steps adapted for those of us who suffered losses, either actual or potential. The program was designed by Dr. Vernon Bittner, Director of the Institute for Christian Living (ICL) in suburban Minneapolis.

I had finished "formal" therapy at ICL and realized I must go on. I needed "lighter" therapy at this point. I knew I had to rebuild my faith, to re-establish trust in God. I didn't like the feeling of doubting God's role in my life.

With my neighbor as my security in the same large room with fifteen others, I felt quite comfortable. Again I realized the magnitude of the burdens some people were carrying. A dying child, a wife in grief; joblessness, hopelessness. I felt selfish. I had a half-time job and could begin full-time employment when I was ready. I had food on my table, a roof over my head, children, parents, friends and neighbors who cared deeply about me. "If I get out of this in one piece," I vowed, "I've got to help others like me." My pain was like real physical pain that doesn't leave. But what must their pain be like? I couldn't imagine.

I left the church building after the last session of Twelve Steps for Christian Living, alone, as usual, but feeling comfortable. As I drove through the evening to my home, I realized I was going to be all right—someday soon I would be all right. I felt better, suddenly, and I was! I was going to be all right! As I turned the corner and looked down the street at my home I felt elation—actual "joy" for the first time in so long. I went into the house and cried and cried, not certain if it was for joy or for sorrow. It must have been a little of each. It felt good.

Twelve Steps for Christian Living was a major key to freedom! After being in women's group therapy for eight months, this healing, spiritual therapy seemed to be the pathway to a new and improved life. Each week after small group discussion, participants would describe their stories and the progress they had made. After one gentleman described his pathway back to healthy life, the facilitator reminded us that each step ahead was a step upwards, illustrating this progress by drawing a diagonal line from lower left to upper right. This graphic illustration made me aware of my progress and set me free to be Me once again. Most importantly, I knew that God would take care of me and this situation. Twelve Steps for Christian Living was like fusion—it brought me back into the fold with total trust in God's wisdom and support.

Abandonment—The Prayer

Although I was eager to renew my spiritual strength through the Twelve Steps for Christian Living program, one session became a stumbling block. Someone handed each of us a printed prayer card and invited us to join in prayer to close the evening's meeting. This was called the Prayer of Abandonment. It was awful! The words stuck in my throat. Abandon myself to Christ? They had to be kidding! How would I handle everything I had to do to get myself well by pretending God could do all of it for me? No way. He hadn't done so well in handling my life. I was exhausted from trying to plan my life and didn't need some fanatic prayer card to foul me up even more! What could I do? I couldn't tell all those people this situation was too "religious" for me. I just read the prayer with them and pretended it meant something to me. How can some people gush all this "godly" talk? It's disgusting at times. Maybe I shouldn't be here.

Satan worked overtime when the prayer card entered my hands. I put the card in my class book, the book was put away and the prayer was forgotten. Nearly two years passed before I saw it again. A friend was interested in reviewing Dr. Bittner's text for the Twelve Steps for Christian Living program, and I offered to share my copy.

I found the prayer card and remembered how it affected me. I sat down and read the prayer and wept tears of joy. I had "said" the prayer several times before, but had never truly "prayed" it. It was like a miracle! This time the words didn't offend me but brought me peace. For by this time I had abandoned my life to Christ, over and over. And He was uplifting me and showering me with blessings.

The Prayer of Abandonment

Father, I abandon myself into your hands.
    Do with me what you will.
Whatever you may do, I thank you;
    I am ready for all, I accept all.
Let only your will be done in me,
    and in all your creatures.
I wish no more than this, O Lord.
Into your hands I commend my soul;
    I offer it to you
    with all the love of my heart,
    for I love you, Lord
    and so need to give myself;
    to surrender myself into your hands,
    without reserve,
    and with boundless confidence,
    for you are my Father.
·Amen

Author unknown

*When I think back to my strong reaction against the prayer, I laugh. Today these words are such a comfort to me. Praying them feels like cocoa and toast on a winter night. I have learned that there is only one way to go, and that is with Him. By abandoning myself to His will, **worry** no longer holds a place in my vocabulary. Yes, there are still concerns in life but allowing God—and only God—to control my life has brought me His peace "...which passes all understanding..."*

Why Did You Leave?

Why did you have to leave? Why? What was so terrible—so horrible—that you would turn your back on all of us, those who loved you so dearly? Forget them for a moment…why did you leave *me*? Can't you just tell me? I feel that because you left me, it must be my fault. I need a good reason. There has to be a *good* reason to cause all of this agony for so many people whom you professed to love. I faintly recall your stating, as you left, that you could not love me the way I deserved to be loved. Why not? What was blocking you for the rest of our years together—until death do us part? We're at our mid-point of life! Now is the time we could celebrate all the years behind us. Now is when we could travel and have fun together. Together—just the two of us.

I've learned to know many new people since you left. Some of them are married, most are not. Some are people who are learning to live again, just as I am. But you wouldn't believe the hell they've gone through. Wanna know something? We lived in Camelot. Yes, I said Camelot. We treated each other so well. You wouldn't believe the way some people were treated—the boundaries they crossed in abusing each other. We didn't experience that kind of life. Ours was charmed in comparison.

Remember how our children said their friends were amazed at us, because we'd never hesitate to hug each other in front of them or their friends? Interesting, isn't it? Those other parents are still together, and we are not.

People who knew us thought we were ideal. Our friend Jim said, "It was as if Dick Van Dyke and Mary Tyler Moore broke up when your marriage ended." He said that! And remember the huge 40th birthday party you gave for me? As my "roast" ended, Patty stood up and said to you, for all those people to hear, "You don't need a fan club; you have Jan." That comment said it all. It spoke to my wifeliness, my total admiration of you as a person and as a very talented sales executive. It affirmed me as the loving wife I truly was. There was lots of kidding that night, but Patty brought seriousness to the event by changing the mood. I will never forget her comment.

Such statements came from our closest friends, people who knew us best. We couldn't fool them if we wanted to. So what went wrong?

It wasn't me at all. It was something within you, wasn't it? Something within you wanted more...or at least the chance to find out if there was indeed more. You went off to live the life of a single man, but it didn't last very long. You didn't like it; you said you were lonely. I know about lonely. And when you entered into a new relationship several months after you left, it wasn't with a young thing who pampered your male ego. You chose someone our age who was caring and sensible.

You wrote to me a few weeks after you left saying you were thinking of returning. You said in your letter, "I know you and I can have the best marriage in the world." Know what? I think we did. To make it better would have been tremendous! But you decided not to return.

I remember when you came back home to visit, three months after you left, as if to test the water. We talked to a counselor that day and he warned you, "Don't throw the baby out with the bath water." I watched your face as you heard those words. They didn't affect you; I could see that. I don't believe you allowed yourself to hear them. You were determined to continue in your quest for newness.

I tell my new friends about you. They're amazed at times that I can compliment you and tell them they would have enjoyed knowing you! I'm glad to share my feelings about you, to let them know who you really are.

Yes, I have chosen to overlook some things that resulted from circumstances beyond your conscious control, from outside influences, and more. That's called unconditional love…even with the scars and the stains. As your hair turned prematurely silver, I loved you even more. You knew that. I told you so.

You were at the core of my life. You made my heart sing! I remember the intimacies, our joy in the fulfillment of rich married love. I remember countless joys, countless victories. I remember trips you won year after year for sales excellence. I remember being so proud of you, so pleased to be introduced as your wife, which made me obviously special to the others. I remember people commenting on something wonderful you said about me. They remarked that it was "cute" to see a husband so proud of his wife. We were good together, really good.

Lee said, "He had it all." I think you did. You had more than most men, and you left it behind.

*My question became a love letter. If we were to pursue the "whys" of life, we could go crazy. We can blame ourselves for everything. I carried shame (thou shalt **not** divorce) for a long period, until therapy sessions helped me recognize that the shame I put upon myself was mere defense. There's an element of emotional abuse in blaming others for responding negatively to our own poor behavior.*

The changes at mid-life make us wonder what we're doing in certain situations. There were times I felt "put upon," that I was being the careful one, and he was oppositely flamboyant. It was a subject we couldn't discuss, because he was right and I was wrong. No contest. Problem? I didn't think so. There was balance in other areas. If we had walked in complete tandem with each other, life could have been very boring.

But we were remiss in our serious conversation. We didn't talk enough about our real feelings. I didn't think much about it then; I do now. I truly didn't think we had to agree on everything, simply because we were two unique individuals. Besides, we didn't disagree on much, so' it didn't appear to be a problem. The '80s brought new insight in couples' communication, in expression of any kind. We were from an era that "put up with" things. Maybe it was better that way. Today we have to analyze every thought. I may think one way today and another tomorrow. Which thought should be my albatross?

I remember the Saturdays we'd take off in the car with the thermos full of coffee and drive for hours, laughing, singing, stopping at a local carnival or art show, eating a late lunch at a small town cafe, arriving home refreshed and renewed late in the evening. We did fun things, many at the spur of the moment. We were good together. People called us a "dynamic" couple. Isn't it interesting?

I remember all that, and all these years later, I still ask, "Why?"

Divorce Granted

Eleven months after he left, I walked across the skyway to the government center to meet my attorney and appear in court, as directed, to request that my divorce be granted. My mind conjured a picture of a court room with a few spectators, perhaps those who might enjoy sitting in on such proceedings. It wasn't that way at all. My attorney led me to an office where a judge sat at a large desk. Photographs of his family adorned the credenza behind him. We were introduced and my attorney excused himself. I'm paying eight hundred dollars for this? There was no contest, no settlement dispute. I felt so cheap, so violated!

The judge quickly reviewed the papers and noted that my birthday would occur in two weeks. He stated that if he signed the documents and let them proceed through normal channels, "It could be your luck to have the divorce actually become final on your birthday." He summoned his clerk and asked her to "walk the papers through" for filing purposes in order that they would be dated November 24 rather than December 4. He then said, "You've been through enough, I'm sure."

The kindness of this gentle man touched me that day. Certainly he saw the dismay on my face, the agony in my eyes. His sensitivity to my plight helped me realize that I was not an undesirable person. Rather, I was to be pitied that day, that last day of my marriage of 29 years. Jan and Jim were no longer. We had been a legend to many, but we were finished. Oh, my God, how could this happen!

My thoughts return to that day from time to time.
I remember being nearly physically unable to walk back
to the office just one block away. I made it back, but left

shortly afterwards to take the bus home. I was immobilized and realized the horrible truth—that it was over. Emotions took their physical toll, and it took a long time to revitalize. My out-of-town family would arrive later that day for Thanksgiving. I had much to do in the kitchen. I wouldn't tell them. They didn't need to know. It would ruin Thanksgiving for everyone.

Stamped in my memory, however, is the judge who expressed warmth and concern for my personal well-being and set a tone of peacefulness to an otherwise horrid day.

It's All in a Name

I despise the word "divorce." I picture a "loose" woman, never a man—always a woman. I envision someone of loose moral character, someone who doesn't care about anyone but herself. My age is showing, I fear, because my images are those from the '50s and '60s, not of the '80s. Divorce today, I'm sorry to say, is all too common. It seems to mean what "breaking up" meant to those "going steady" in my teenage years. Certainly we have the freedom of choice. But without a Biblical marriage, there is no concern for continuity—for longevity. If it doesn't work, we replace it. If it breaks, we throw it out.

It didn't feel good to say, "After I was divorced…"
I preferred to say, "When I was first alone…"

From This Day Forward

While reading about how to rebuild my life, I got a real jolt. The author said, "Real healing does not begin until the day of the divorce!" Thanks a lot! That means all the misery I went through from Christmas until the following Thanksgiving was for naught? I went through my first Christmas alone, a few weeks after the divorce was final, and nearly fell to pieces! The author further stated, "With the divorce papers in your hand, you no longer foster false hopes of reconciliation. You know you're single again, and you're equipped to live accordingly."

Sure, I thought. I could barely drag myself home the day our divorce became final. I had never known my physical being to be so drained of everything it had contained.

As if I could just say, "We're divorced now. Thank you very much for all those years. See ya. Neeexxxt!" Who writes these books, anyway? And who do they use for models? Actors? How can anyone who has been married so long to someone she loved just turn that page in life and step right into another phase—without trauma?

That day, I decided I must be very weak. I must be one major case! There is no way that I can, even after being divorced just three months, pick up and go on as if nothing ever happened. If it's written in books, it must be kind of true. I'm getting better every day, but how on earth will I *ever* be right again?

David left on a business trip early Sunday afternoon. Denise called and asked if I'd join her for an early dinner at a favorite restaurant. I was delighted! Sundays can be so miserable, but now I could spend the

entire afternoon anticipating our dinner. I love being with Denise. She's a daughter/sister all in one. She is understanding and warm. I'm so lucky to have her in my family.

I told her what I had read about growth, and about being generally concerned with the time already spent rebuilding. I was fearful of how much more time it would take. I actually felt that I had made no progress and now I'd have to return to "Go" and try to make it all the way to Boardwalk in one play. The year of separation anticipating divorce had been the most ungodly miserable time I had ever spent. To consider all that time wasted, to say that "it didn't count" in the growth process, was unthinkable.

Denise listened for a short time, but suddenly her eyes began to dance and she got a delightful smile on her face. "Janice Marie, (my children use my full name as my nickname when they're humoring me) look at yourself! Don't you know how far you've come? Haven't you looked in the mirror? Don't you remember how you looked last year? You were always so tired. Now you've got energy and you're doing lots of things. I'm just so proud of you and all you've accomplished! Both David and I are terribly proud of you."

It is good, really good, to hear about your own progress as seen through the eyes of another. Each day, sometimes each hour, is an effort. We don't notice the mini-changes as they occur. We're tired from working so hard at existing, at learning how to live again.

It takes lots of mini-changes to make a noticeable change; but, like funds saved with accruing interest, one day it is noticeable and we're happy with the progress.

Questions

How do you answer the questions of others? Especially those of little children. Five-year-old Lindsey asked, "Tell me what happened when Grampa left. Why did he leave, anyway, Gramma? Did you have a fight?" Her expressive eyes looked at me with such concern. I was amazed at the sensitivity of this little girl. My heart nearly broke when I looked into Lindsey's beautiful face as she waited for my answer. Erik was three. He stood next to her, his wide, brown eyes looking at me with intense seriousness, expecting an exciting, blow-by-blow description.

I knew then that I had to give a good answer and give the same answer, always. "Grampa decided he wanted to start a new life, so he left."

That's all they needed. Just an answer.

These children, these beautiful little children! They love their Grampa so much, and he loves them even more. He's cheated himself out of this moment when two little treasures would come with wide, dark eyes and ask such an important question. I wanted to say "Your Grampa's a jerk!" but I couldn't, and I **wouldn't.** *Their Grampa and I are parents of their mother, our first wonderful child. How could I hate him, when I look into the faces of these children?*

He missed so much of the joy of watching them grow. They've missed many joyful times with a doting "grandpa." How very sad!

Running Away

I can't stand being here. There's nothing to do. I don't feel like "keeping house." No one is here but me. Who cares? Besides, leaving it messy will give me something to do all day on Saturday.

I went to Karel and Dale's tonight. It's the second time this week I've visited my daughter and her husband. They're always glad to see me—I think. Karel is sensitive to my aloneness, and Dale is always so gracious to me. I'm glad they live nearby.

I just have to go over there to sit on the sofa and hold Dylan. He's so cute and cuddly, and he lets me rock him and sing to him. He'll sit on my lap to watch television and doesn't mind being hugged and kissed. It really helps to be able to touch someone, to connect.

There were weeks that I wasn't in my home one evening. It was miserable to be there, just as it was miserable to be any place. I was fortunate these children of mine understood my feelings. I didn't discuss it with them, but they seemed to know how I felt.

Dylan became very special to me at this time. He was the first little one born after I was alone, and it seemed strange to have no one to celebrate with when the call came announcing his birth. He was always there to satisfy my need to touch, to hold and to give love.

Now I'm back in the mode of a happy homemaker again! I love taking care of my home, making it pleasant and cozy. It's a good nest for me and all those who enjoy it with me!

What is Lost

People make the strangest comments in an attempt to make me feel better. "At least he didn't die," or "Too bad he didn't die."

I'm glad he didn't die. We all need him to complete the family, even if the family doesn't join hands in one complete circle. He's here in the faces of my children who resemble both of us, physically and intellectually.

My friends *have* lost their spouses to death. Jerry's wife and Renee's husband died of cancer. I didn't know either of them before we became single again. We all experienced similar pain and all of us have worked very hard to return to the stream of life.

Divorce causes financial problems that can be devastating. Thank goodness I have my retirement savings program working for me. I was granted my home (together with its mortgage payment book and other encumbrances). There is no life insurance for divorce, so I have no cushion in the bank to fall back on. It's scary. It's up to me to make it work.

I rejected divorce for several months, but when he announced his plans to remarry, there was no hope, no need to hang on. I wanted it to be over quickly. Because I agreed to work in haste to end the marriage, I cheated myself out of potential additional income. Some women are supported forever! I felt at times that my years as a wife were worth nothing if I were to put a dollar value on years of service.

For the first months after the divorce became final, it was difficult to realize that settlement money would be sent for only one year. I was upset with its limitations and frightened to think of truly "going it alone." I needed to be so frugal, so very careful—forever.

If he had died, I'd have enough money. He was keenly aware of the need for adequate insurance coverage. Perish the thought! I didn't want him dead. He will always be a loving father and grandfather. But managing alone is scary.

What About Me?

I am so angry I could scream! Today is New Year's Eve, 1988, and he's back in our area with his bride, all set to have a combination Christmas/New Year's celebration with the kids tonight. Kris and Mike and the children are here with me and they'll stay the weekend. They've said they'd bring the little kids back to my house tonight so I could put them to bed and the adults can stay up as late as they want. There's nothing for me to do tonight, so it will be fun to get the little ones into bed, fun to have someone else in the house with me.

Why did he have to come to town now? Does he have to continue to ruin my holidays? The kids are excited to see him, and it disgusts me. He can run away and ruin everything, and they're breaking their necks to see him.

I made cranberry pudding, with the sauce to match, and sent it with the kids for their dessert. It's a tradition from his side of the family that I adopted many years ago. It wouldn't be Christmas without it, and it was their Christmas celebration, after all. That made me angry, too. Why was I still trying to keep everyone happy? I wanted to keep our family and its traditions together. Somehow I had to keep trying.

I was angry that he was in town, angry with the kids for playing into his hand and celebrating Christmas with him, when they knew I'd never have another peaceful Christmas again. I was angry that I'd be home alone. There he is—he wasn't alone at all. He covered his feelings, then found her and developed a relationship and married, all in a very short time. I don't want the kids to know how I feel. I know it sounds selfish but I can't help it. His timing is all wrong. He used to be so considerate and now he's all for himself!

Evening came, the kids left, and I became angrier and angrier, very aware it was New Year's Eve, watching the neighbors drive away to the dinner party they had been anticipating for weeks. Is this the way it's going to be? Will I always be stuck here with nothing to do on New Year's Eve?

Lindsey and I sat on the sofa in the darkened living room. She didn't want to go to bed after her parents brought her and the other children home to sleep. She wanted to see what New Year's midnight looked like. The night skies were clear and the stars shone brightly. The snow sparkled. It was a pretty sight. She was in her pajamas and smelled sweet, as a little girl should. As she nestled with me on the sofa, I asked her about the evening with her Grampa and his wife. They were probing questions that she'd answer innocently without realizing I was probing. I wanted to hear that he was unhappy, that the evening was a "bust." Nothing of the sort. Everyone was happy, the gifts were abundant.

Then it hit me, like a bolt out of the midnight sky. Wasn't this just about enough? Hadn't I agonized long enough? Now that he was married, why did I continue to long for him and for the family we once were? That was it. No more. I vowed then and there that tomorrow would be the first day of a new and different life.

On Mountain Paths
3

He leadeth me
in the paths of righteousness
...my cup runneth over. Psalm 23:3,5

On My Knees

Joni is a special friend. She is good for my soul. We worked together in my first position after moving to Minneapolis. She is several years younger than I am, a Christian with a strong Roman Catholic faith. Stephen, her husband, contracted Hodgkins Disease as a young man and has had surgery, radiation and chemotherapy to halt the progress. Their strong faith has held them up, and they glorify God and tell of His strength in their lives whenever there is an opportunity. Joni and Stephen are the "beautiful" people. Both are strikingly attractive and have outgoing, radiant personalities. On the outside, one wouldn't guess their lives have been marked by the ravages of disease and fear.

My own therapy had been difficult, but I began to develop a sense of well-being in the knowledge that one day I would be well again. It would take more time. I was impatient and didn't want to hurt any longer. I was sick and tired of working so hard to accomplish everything I did. One day, I told Joni about my feelings. She admonished me, matter of factly, with a lilt in her voice, "You'll just have to give it up by asking God to take it from you. He promised He'd take your burdens. You know that! So you just get down on your knees and tell him how you feel! Ask Him to take charge of your life!"

I got on my knees, night after night, at the side of my bed and begged God to help me, to take the pain away and to make everything better for me. Several weeks passed, and I hadn't felt a great sense of relief. I asked Joni, "How long will this take?" Joni's answer was strong. "Until you've convinced Him you're serious." She told me I had to truly believe it myself—I had to *truly* release my burdens to His will. As in repeating a daily affirmation, I had to be sincere in relinquishing control to God's power. Night after night I went about my business of convincing God I *was* serious. I needed to give Him the reins of my life and let go of them myself.

Joy came in the morning! The night before, in a state of desperation, I got on my knees at the side of the bed and admonished God, if He was indeed in Heaven, to remove the burden from my heart and soul—forever.

The next morning, as if by a miracle, I awakened relieved of the emotional pain that had haunted me for the past two years. It was as if I had been reborn into a new world. I was ready to accept healing. I wanted it so badly.

Little by little, I could feel myself allowing the control to pass from myself into God's will. Surrendering, abandoning all, brought me into a new life process that will direct my life forever. A new peace surrounded me. It was a knowledge that if I continued to let go He would bring new vistas into my life that I wouldn't dream possible. It became exciting—it became an adventure! Therapy had been successful. Now I was tasting the frosting on the cake!

During the next weeks and months, that joy was noticed by others, especially my friends with whom I worked every day. Many of them were plagued with ongoing problems. Filled with joy at my new peacefulness, it had become easy for me to talk with them and share my story; to tell them, without reservation, that I had abandoned my life to Christ and had put myself totally in His will. I was so happy. Because I loved them so, I wanted them to be happy as well.

One day my friend Carolyn said, "I think I know why God allowed this to happen. He *knew* you'd be a minister to us, for Him."

Carolyn's comment made an impact on my life. I had healed well enough to know that sometimes God allows things to happen to us in order to accomplish

greater purposes. To have been called a "minister" was a great honor, and that was only the first time sharing my story has brought blessing and realization to others. Like an earthly father, our Heavenly Father pours gifts upon His children. When He sees the joy in His children, He, like an earthly father, wants to give us even more. He saw the joy in me and has continued to bless me with many new gifts. I have gladly given up the fear, the worry, the discontentment that plagued me for such a long time. When it creeps back, it is simply a matter of asking for help—on my knees.

We have a duty, I believe, to be His disciples, bringing light and hope where darkness had otherwise presided. Now I was empowered to be a light.

I recalled a Bible verse memorized in fifth grade.

"And I am sure that he who began a good work in you will bring it to completion at the day of Jesus Christ." (Philippians 1:6)

Friends are Friends...
Forever

Friendship is such a healing relationship. My old friends are extra-special. Others are newer friends, of all ages.

Through the years, friendships grew stronger and stronger. And when I needed those friends, they were there for me—stronger than ever.

Some new friends are members of my singles group at church. Eight of us on our planning team spent lots of time together in meetings and on committees. It often seemed we were just trying to find reasons to get together. After several weeks, it was apparent we were bonding to each other. We became a family.

Marty, Renee and I became especially close friends. We've shared big and little victories in our lives and worked hard to bring ourselves into emotional health. It has been hard work for all of us; the bond of friendship ensured that someone was always there for us, no matter what time of day or night.

And then there's my long-time co-worker, Gloria. She's a bright spot in my life each day. At lunch together, we laugh and change our focus from the working world. We share similar interests and have fun dreaming about our futures.

Karen and I became friends as young mothers. Now our little granddaughters are friends.

Many years ago, Bonnie and I left our respective northern Minnesota homes for the big city, where we met and became roommates. She was the maid of honor at my wedding. We have history in our friendship which makes it very special. We're like sisters.

ᖍ

Each of us needs a special friend, a mentor who can hear us when we cry out for help and rejoice with us when we have a victory. We each need someone who will listen and share on a regular basis. Close friendships bless us. Friends lean on each other and support each other as they continue to grow. Friends listen attentively to each other, pray with and for each other, and generally support and dearly love each other.

Male friends are a new phenomenon to me. Many are like brothers. They add a new dimension to my life. They are caring and loving, concerned and protective. They're also intelligent and diversified, which makes them interesting and attractive.

Some of the first people to come forward with outstretched arms and hearts were these precious old friends. They were "our" friends, and it was difficult for them. They weren't concerned with details. They were concerned for our well-being—for both of us. Fortunately, I was the one close enough to benefit from this outpouring of love.

Used as an Angel

The first summer I was alone I decided to travel to Holden Village, a Lutheran retreat center in the Cascade Mountains. I felt the need to get away, to be in nature, to hide from the world. God had other things in mind. I didn't realize I was sent there for a purpose.

A lovely older couple befriended me immediately. They were concerned about my aloneness. After days of visiting, the man told me he had lost his job as a professor in a prominent school. He also had lost his self-respect. Now he was suffering from embarrassment, false pride and other painful emotions. We talked about our situations and it seemed we were ministering to each other.

On the day they left, he told me I had surely been sent to Holden to help him. "You're an angel," he said, "God sent you here to be my angel." His comment surprised me. I felt honored—truly honored—because I then realized I had been used to help someone else.

When I was first alone I promised, "God, if you help me, I'll help others." I knew I was healing, because God was using me already! It was so exciting. I felt as if I had been blessed with a special gift. I've heard about the gifts of the Holy Spirit. Had I been given one of them?

Through the years, this same scenario has repeated itself several times. People have shared their concerns, their stories. We've talked about bringing our problems to the foot of the cross in prayer, about handing over our problems to Christ thereby freeing ourselves to live according to His will, not our own.

I felt that I had a right, as a disciple put in that place, to ask such questions. The response has always been positive and has repeated itself from the ski resorts of Montana to the office in which I work.

Release on the Mountaintop

After-dinner conversation at Holden Village was animated and varied. By mid-week, it was fun to go into the dining hall for meals. Several people made certain I would sit with them. It felt good to be sought out! Afterwards, I went alone to the ice cream shop to get a chocolate cone and visit with others. Several young couples with little children were there. They knew I was alone and went out of their way to befriend me and include me. I needed to return their friendship by seeking them out. I sat on the ledge of the deck and visited with them. I affirmed their parenting skills. I simply cherished being with them. They told me they enjoyed my company, that they appreciated my constant smile. (They didn't realize I was smiling in amazement!)

A small group was discussing tomorrow's hike to the top of Holden Mountain. I was intrigued, but I didn't plan to go. Nevertheless, it was interesting to hear the men talk about it. I had always enjoyed the out of doors—that's why I was here! As a little child I loved to run and climb. Although I was an observer, I truly (perhaps secretly) wished to be a participant.

Jerry and his young son, Erik, were planning an early morning departure. The hike is five miles up, five miles down. A series of switchbacks makes the climb tolerable for novices. Someone in the group said, "Jan, you're planning to go, aren't you?" "Yes," I said, "I'm going!" I was amazed at my answer!

"What?" I asked myself. "What's going on?"

Suddenly I had a strong urge—a feeling of RELEASE! It was as if the old person broke away and the new person emerged. I became very excited and began discussing the climb with Jerry. Carl, who had become my friend, warned me that it is very tiring for a novice. He warned me about the flies in the underbrush near the top, about shin splints on the climb down, and the overpowering heat of the noonday sun high on the mountain. He neglected to warn me about the sweet experiences ahead!

I met Jerry and Erik at the starting point, equipped with sandwiches, fruit, and a full water bottle. It would not be a long day, but a tiring morning. Carl was waiting to walk with me the first quarter mile, to the point of ascent. He warned me that I should not overdo and pull muscles that had not been used before. He explained that there is no harm in stopping, in returning to the base point. The more he talked, the more determined I became. I was heading up the mountain, and I would reach the summit!

I walked behind Jerry and Erik, amazed at the beauty of the Cascades. Flowering bushes provided a soft frame for the sight of the majestic peaks surrounding us. Soon we were high enough to look down into the valley where our little Holden Village lay in all its serenity. My strength didn't waiver—it was amazing. I felt like The Little Engine That Could, except that my chant was "I know I can...I know I can!"

As we came off the last switchback and walked to the clearing at the end of the trail, the summit, I was stunned by the sight of the clear crystal lake, the ice and snow on the far peak, the deer frolicking in the meadow. Others were there, having come from another side of the Cascade chain. I was thankful I wore sunglasses, because my tears were flowing heavily. *This* is the mountaintop experience! I was overwhelmed with joy. I made it! I really made it! I wanted to make it; I wanted so badly to make it. I have the strength, the stamina. If I can do this, I can do anything!! I had not only accomplished *this* mountaintop—it was as if I had conquered the Mt. Everest of life!

We had just a short time to eat our lunch and begin the downward trek. I ate quickly and walked a short ways to find a mountain stream edged with rocks and flowering trees. It was exciting to plan a photograph, to decide the layout. Everything was exciting today! This was the beginning—another new and wonderful beginning!

From this experience on Holden Mountain, it suddenly seemed that I could accomplish anything. I didn't want to be like everyone else. I was a risk-taker—I dared to be different. I was keenly aware (perhaps since the shocking death of my brother in 1963) that we only have so much time on earth and if we are going to experience life, we'd better get on with it!

After my trip to Holden Village, I yearned for more new things. I made a mental list. I began to say "yes" more readily. Anne Marie asked me to accompany her when she went to Sweden the next year to buy a new car. We would drive to Oslo to visit her brother, the Bishop of Norway, and stay at his home a few days. "Okay," I said, "and I'll fly over to the west coast of Norway and visit **my** *family for a few days." As we completed the conversation, I felt like a million dollars! "All right!" I said to myself. "This is something I want to do. I have a year to plan how I'm going to save the money, and I'm going to go!"*

We can put up all kinds of barriers, make all kinds of excuses, none of which will accomplish our goals. I've learned to say YES, to go with my instincts and to live the avant-garde life.

Bottom line—I'm being Me!

Singles—A New Ministry

One of my greatest frustrations was the church's inability (or so it seemed to me) to face the fact that much of its membership consists of single-parent families or people like me, who were suddenly single again.

A new era in family life exists today. It is a sad time, with so many broken families in our society. The church must be equipped to minister to all people, regardless of family status. We must do all we can to help individuals regain the self-esteem that is so easily lost in the conflict.

Janice is a member of my church who works at my office. She discussed her membership on our Family Life Committee with me. She asked if I would be interested in being nominated to replace her unexpired term on the committee.

"But I'm divorced! How can I belong to the committee that establishes programs for families within our church family?" She saw no problem; neither did the church council.

Just a few months later, after listening to program plans involving parents and children, I expressed concern that there were also people like me—people who had once been a "family" but were single again. Were we ministering to our single adults? Perhaps there were also younger people, single parents with children at home, and others who needed the same educational advantages as those we provided for married couples with children. The committee changed its focus to investigate new methods of ministry. I was pleased to be involved, because I felt compelled to champion the cause for this new phase of ministry in our congregation.

Five years after my need to lean on my church, I am working with our pastors and committees to create a

wholesome Christian environment for single adults and their children.

Now church "feels" so good. It is wonderful to feel welcome, to know everyone cares so much about all of us who find ourselves single again.

Several of us who are single again are leaders in evangelism and parish care ministries in our congregation. This represents a phenomenal change in the church's views toward divorced individuals in leadership roles. We are committed leaders because we have walked the walk and realize the needs of the soul in transition. Our mission includes the entire family of God and is no longer reserved "for singles only."

Forgiveness

Part of our responsibility as members of the Family Life Committee at church was to take an active role in the selection and presentation of video series based on problems encountered by modern families. I was to introduce the presentation on children in broken families and how they often are "used" by their parents as pawns. I was also asked to lead a brief discussion following the video.

One gentleman and a room full of women viewed the video one Sunday morning. Many of the women were young. The discussion broke into a period of "husband-bashing," where the women vented their anger. Unresolved issues filled the air.

The last comment came from the lone man in the room who, with tears in his eyes, asked why the children have to be used. "Why do women feel it is necessary to fill the children with the anger they feel?" He told about his heartbreak at the loss of visitation rights with his only son. My heart seemed to snap apart as I realized the truth in his question. "Why, indeed?" I thought. The children are already suffering from actions they probably do not understand. How do the children feel when they hear horrible things about the absent parent whom they also love? Where is their allegiance supposed to be?

This event was a major turning point in my life.

When I arrived at home after the Sunday presentation, I was disconcerted with the scene that occurred just hours before. Perhaps my former husband feels this way. Perhaps he, too, is broken hearted at the distance between him and our children. Surely he misses them. I pictured him with tears flowing down his cheeks, and it saddened me. I realized then that I had not yet forgiven *him. While working through Twelve Steps for Christian Living, I had had difficulty with the step involving forgiveness. I had set it aside for another day.*

The day had come. Today was the day. I stood in the living room and looked out onto the yard bathed in sunshine and said his name out loud followed by the words "...I forgive you. What you did to me is terrible, but I forgive you. I know you didn't mean for me to suffer the rest of my life—and I won't—and I forgive you today and every day, for the rest of my life!"

This "ceremony of forgiveness" was one of the most essential points in my growth. It freed me still more to continue my progress, my uphill climb.

My heart reached out to the man at church who touched my life so profoundly that day. Although I often looked for him to express my gratitude and concern, three years passed before I met him again.

We're Single Again

So much time had passed since I had been anywhere socially with anyone but my children. There must be others out there, others in my church, who had suffered the same aloneness that I encountered.

I asked permission at a Family Life Committee meeting to work out a plan to re-establish a singles group for people in my age group. (A previous singles organization at our church had dissolved.) I needed to meet good, solid Christian people and believed this was the avenue to take. Permission was granted.

Our first meeting was attended by several women and a few men. It was an informal meeting with no agenda. We talked about our situation and all agreed we had had enough therapy. We wanted to socialize; Renee commented that she hadn't eaten at a restaurant with a tablecloth since her husband passed away. I related to her comment, so we decided to organize and plan social events.

Nearly four years have passed at this writing. The membership now includes more than 200 people! We've had wonderful, meaningful experiences in learning to live as single people. It is more apparent than ever that God, in His goodness, put all of us together for a purpose. Our lives have been enhanced, enriched, brightened, and made joyful. The social interaction with others in my situation provided me with a gift that helped me heal.

We've grown individually; we have bonded as a small group of original planners and have enjoyed so many new experiences. As we develop confidence in ourselves again and move out into the world, we do so with a stronger faith and the knowledge that we are not alone.

Laughter

Six "mature" adults from the singles group at church climbed into my compact station wagon like teenagers and headed out to a pre-July 4th evening celebration. We brought supper and sat on blankets in the midst of a crowded park. After the fireworks, we returned to the car, which had been parked with many others in a farm field. Dennis decided we should drive through the field onto a nearby shopping center parking lot rather than attempt to move with the slow traffic onto the street. With me at the wheel, guided by Leon's able direction, the car became mired in mud up to the hub caps. We worked together as a team, three men and three women, finding a post to work as a crow bar to boost the car and twigs and branches to create traction under the tires. It was a dark evening, the moon provided the only light. Cal took the wheel (he was wearing white trousers). Renee, Marty and I helped the men push the car, the tires spraying mud on our summer whites and pastels. We laughed uproariously—so hard that we had to rest from time to time to catch our breath.

We returned to our meeting point to exchange cars and hose our feet and legs with water. We took a few photographs and went on our way. I knew that if my children had come home in such condition I would have had them tested for illegal chemicals!

I've always loved to laugh, but I didn't realize its therapeutic value. The "fun" became even more fun because we were men and women together, but boys and girls at heart. It was exciting and new. In this long process of healing, the seriousness of discussion becomes overwhelming in its depth. It's vital to "lighten up," to see the humor in life and enjoy it. It's free!—and it feels sooooo good!

Heavenly Sunshine

My friend Cal and I attended a Sunday evening gospel music festival at a neighboring church and came away thrilled with the possibility of developing a gospel music singing group. Our past experiences, his in vocal music and mine as an organist and accompanist, qualified us to dream of such a ministry.

I invited the planning team of our singles group to Sunday supper at my home. It was winter; a good time to spend an evening with good friends and good food.

The piano stood in my home as a memorial to a past life. Music no longer was the focal point of my home. But now my guests were members of the choir at church; all were good singers. I placed a gospel music hymnal on the piano and opened to the old hymn "Heavenly Sunshine." As they sang, I quipped, "You could be called the Heavenly Sunshine Singers!" That day was the beginning of a wonderful era in our lives.

As we met regularly in my home to sing together, a new ministry of music was born. We organized Sunday evening services we called Second Sunday Singspirations. Cal led these events as worship leader and director of the Heavenly Sunshine Singers. I served as accompanist. These Singspirations continued for nearly two years.

We still meet for rehearsals and prepare music for occasional performances during regular worship services at our church. Through this ministry, life seemed to come full circle. My dream of new involvement in music had been realized.

I felt God truly sought us for this special ministry. The blessings of sharing our music are unsurpassed.

The Awakening

The return of music to my life came with a sense of amazement. It seems unbelievable that it would come so suddenly, without plan. One day my piano receives the obligatory dusting; the next day it is covered with music books and it's badly in need of tuning! The gift of music is one of the greatest, most welcome gifts I have ever received. I play the piano in the morning, in the evening, even in the middle of the night when I cannot sleep. It brings me such joy. It makes me forget my situation and gives me a new incentive to perfect my skills. I am able to pick up where I left off so many years before. Strangely, I am now able to play "by ear," which I had never done before.

Music brings me a sense of vitality, of creativity. I am excited about life! I am awakened!

Music is the universal language. For me, it was the language of life. I had been empty—now I'm filled with a new sense of the beauty of life. I am now aware of the great value of the gifts I am being given.

Music was not the only gift. New opportunities presented themselves. In my new-found vitality, I was suddenly aware there was much to do in this world.

Life became fun! I began to enjoy new activities and involvements with a fervor I could not believe. My energy level climbed to an all-time high. I wanted to run to make up for lost time, to do things I had not done since I was a teenager. It was amazing to me at first, but I knew my prayers were being answered. I was being given another chance at this life, and this time I was going to take advantage of every opportunity.

This flurry of activity came with its own gift. Because I was involved in happy things, I did not have time or desire to think back on unhappy things. Soon the happiness in my life was reflected in my demeanor. Memories of the past were an intrusion. Although it was still necessary to work through some of the emotions caused from the events that changed my life, it was an easier process. I had a strong desire to take on this new life, and my efforts matched that desire.

I was encouraged by the youth pastor at my church to become involved in youth ministry, an involvement that has become one of the brightest parts of my new life.

Life had come back—gift-wrapped—as a treasure from Heaven. I was excited! Life was beginning all over again. Something within me had reawakened!

Jesus said, "I have come that you may have Life, and have it abundantly!" Oh, how true!

Conflicting Feelings

My friend Marty and I co-chaired the spiritual growth emphasis for our singles group. One of our responsibilities was to alternate preparing a monthly article for our group's newsletter, sharing our concepts of this new life and our role in it.

The newsletter became an outlet for the feelings I hadn't dealt with, totally, and the new, sometimes conflicting, feelings I was encountering. New experiences were entering my life. This being single "is not all it's cracked up to be," as Mother would say. People would make nice comments about the articles I wrote, and I'd simply respond, "Thank you, I'm glad you enjoyed it," but that's not what I was really feeling.

"Thank you very much. I was so darned angry with him for making Christmas such a miserable time!"

"Thanks for describing that place!" someone might say about my trip to Holden Village. "It sounds so nice." But I hadn't wanted to go to Holden Village. I forced that trip on myself to avoid a miserable summer at home, alone. I'd have preferred a romantic trip with someone I considered very wonderful.

"You're welcome—but I really wanted to describe someplace on the North Shore of Lake Superior, at the wide point where the opposite shore is not visible; where we could sit for days and just think, just ponder, just find peace again." I think at times I am the incurable romantic—unreasonably so. I want to go "up the Shore," but I don't want to be alone. I want someone there with me to make the fire, to pour the wine. I'd just be there because I'm the perfect person in some wonderful man's mind. He wouldn't even dream (it <u>never</u> enters his head!) that there is anyone but me in his whole, wide, vast, wonderful world. So we sit there and talk for

hours, perhaps days, and we think alike and love all the same things and know we will be soul mates forever.

Then the bubble bursts and I'm just saying, "Thanks for enjoying my description of Holden Village. I loved that place. I'd really like to return there some day."

On Being Religious

In reading these pages you may say, "I'm not as religious as she is." I understand you perfectly. I don't believe anything "turned me off" more than people who said, "God will take care of you," or "Just have faith in God." I felt bitter and angry towards God at first. He took real good care of me, didn't He? How could I ever have real, honest faith in Him again?

Through the anxiety and misery of any horrible situation, it seems natural to blame God. And I *was* angry at what I thought God had done to me. But, I was raised in a Christian home with a grandmother next door who helped prepare a solid foundation under my faith. My faith grew gradually. It was solid, but I had not realized how deep it really was.

The night I got on my knees for the umpteenth time and begged God to take all the hurts from me—to keep them from me—I did so in absolute despair. It was a last-ditch effort. I felt I had to have release. If not, I wondered how I could go on.

The release I felt after that experience convinced me that there truly is a living Christ. I needed to know that, to feel His presence. That knowledge was a great comfort and freed me—literally freed me!—to move on and live my life.

Do I live this "religious" life now? Yes, I do. I begin every day with a prayer of thanksgiving. I ask God to let me feel His presence in my life and ask Him to fill me with the Holy Spirit. That's my insurance and insulation for each new day. I don't go about as a missionary trying to save the world, but I don't hesitate to share my faith and what it has meant, and now means, to me. Those who know me well know I went through my own personal hell. When they marvel at my recovery, I give credit where credit is due.

❦

*I told my children that it wasn't **me** who accomplished healing, it was Christ at work in my life. This is the greatest gift I could give to my family—a living example of Christ's love happening right before their eyes.*

I am active in my church, but I'm also active in the community and other activities that give me a balanced life. I laugh a lot and am obviously a happy person. My standards are high; my moral values are high.

Satan delights in putting barriers in our lives to prevent us from walking to the light. Facing Satan head on frightens him away; God provides us with additional strength. Christ has provided us with all the armor we need to face our adversary.

When concerns come into my life, I take the advice of my friend who suggested we ask, "What would Jesus do?" That admonition makes it quite simple.

Am I religious? Yes!

I Don't Want to Go!

Everyone is going to a play tonight. Deanne arranged for a block of seats at center front. The play has had rave reviews for weeks. I'm not going. I don't feel like going. And I don't have to go if I don't want to! I have felt adamant about this all day. I'm not in the mood. The play is supposed to be humorous. I don't feel like laughing. I'll have to make up some excuse for not attending. What will I say? Every negative decision brings on its own set of problems. I'll just say I don't feel well. Physically, I'm just fine. Emotionally, I just don't feel like going anywhere.

So I stayed home, snuggled under an afghan, and watched TV. I felt guilty not going along with my friends, guilty for enjoying this time by myself.

I usually attended every singles-group event planned. I was in charge of most of the events when our group was new, so I really had no choice. It's like force-feeding; and, like feeding, it did have nutritive value. When we push ourselves to become involved, we find new people and new experiences. But sometimes I didn't feel like being with the same people all the time. I think it's okay to stay home once in a while.

I have stayed home from an event which I thought could be dull and later have heard how others enjoyed it. On the other hand, it's been good to treat myself to a leisurely evening in the bathtub with candlelight and soft music.

We can't be all things to all people. Sometimes we have to stop and take care of ourselves. In the process of healing, we appreciate others and are kind and good to them. We must remember to treat ourselves in the same manner.

What's Going On?!

Why do I feel this way? Everything in my life is going reasonably well. But today I'm lonely...I'm so miserably lonely! Is it depression? How can I be "up" for so long—for months—and then crash so low? Every emotion I have is alive! The relationship that didn't work out jumps back into my mind. Maybe there's a chance for it now. Why do I feel this way? Why am I so busy? Is it because I'm afraid to be alone with myself? It's a circle, isn't it? It's a crazy circle. "For heaven's sake, Jan, don't dwell on this stuff," my rational mind says to my irrational self. "I want to—something very strange within me wants to dwell on this stuff!" It's sick, isn't it? I'll call Bonnie! I can tell her how I feel and she won't be amazed. But she is. "How can you be so up and let something like *this* get you down? Everything is going so well for you! Come on, Jan!" My voice cracks and it's difficult to talk, to answer her. I'm feeling sorry for myself, just like a little child who wants her way.

Nothing seems right. Nothing.

I wonder how things can change so dramatically. Was it a bad day at work? Was it something lacking in my diet or exercise that caused my chemistry to tip out of balance and initiate such an outburst? The sun hasn't shone for two weeks. That doesn't help.

I remember when I was first alone and working hard to get my life back into sync. It was a chaotic period of healing. Every three or four weeks I'd crash to the depths of despair. Time wore on, and the crashes were spaced further and further apart. Perhaps it is not unusual for a person, in life's normal cycle, to fall into despair from time to time. It's not a pleasant place to be. It serves just one purpose. It makes the other days so sweet.

The Boot Strap Syndrome

My old friend Bunny Bailey said, "…Sometimes we just have to pull ourselves up by our boot straps and move on." Wiser words were never spoken! They came out of a discussion over twenty years ago, and I think of them on many occasions when I am readying myself to give up.

People use all kinds of words in identifying their problems. Like the word "dysfunctional." Who invented that word, anyway? Everything is dysfunctional, it seems. Families are dysfunctional, my car surely is at times. The front yard infested with "creeping Charlie" certainly is dysfunctional, and so are my leaky, breezy windows! So whose fault is it anyway? Do we care? Will it do us much good to know? I think back on Bunny's "boot strap" wisdom.

If new experiences reveal dysfunctions in our childhood family, will we reject family members as useless or unworthy? Or will we be able to use the love instilled by Christ within each of us and remember—then forgive— whatever was dysfunctional, whatever affected us. The knowledge that dysfunction occurred in our lives makes us common, one to another, as human beings. The grace given to us through Christ's love sets us apart to love, rather than find fault.

I don't believe we should use our upbringing as an "excuse" for problems in our life. Some situations in our past don't fully reveal themselves. We get little "peeks" into the past, but the mind has a way of shutting that window before we have a chance to remember things fully. Is it the mind protecting us from unpleasant memories? Surely this is true.

*It's easiest to give up! We get tired, we become
disgusted, we become weary. Anyone can give up. It*

takes guts to continue. It takes all we have, sometimes, to get out of bed and declare the beginning of another miserable day. But we **do** have the equipment, the God-given ability to continue. It's left to us—to our own discretion. I believe it's better to move on, to try again.

I have a friend who has overcome a horrible past by "pulling up her boots" and marching directly to therapy, continuing as she sees fit. She tried to pry that window open and could only do so through therapy. She was released into a new and better world! I admire her so. Therapy is absolutely essential, whether therapy or counseling is obtained through a private therapist, a county human services center, or the church. The end result is well worth it.

Rebuilding

I feel as if I were grabbing at something nearly out of reach and have to strain myself with umpteen tons of energy to get hold of it. I sometimes feel as if I'm white-knuckling a brick wall and have to chin myself to the top, just a few inches away, to get over the wall! And it's so difficult—so terribly difficult—to make it that little distance up and over the top. On the other side of that wall is Victory. It's too difficult today. I'll have to do it tomorrow. I hate myself for delaying the attempt. "For goodness sake, Jan, can't you just release all of this and get over the top?"

This stage of rebuilding was not easy. I had great expectations for myself and seemed to let myself down often. I had worked so hard, so very very hard, and I wanted it to be over! I wanted to wake up "all put together," without a concern for the future. My wish was unrealistic and I knew that, but who cares? I didn't. I wanted all of this to be over. Period.

Don't Be Unevenly Yoked

Men were not interesting to me at first. Although I worked with impressive men and enjoyed their intellectual verbal exchanges, those I admired most were married to terrific women. Besides, it couldn't be possible that I would ever know another man who fit into my life as well as my husband had. We grew through all our middle years together; raised our children, had similar backgrounds and ideals, and shared commonalties that can only come from years of living together.

Who would ever take his place in the kitchen and in the dining room when we entertained? Who would ask me, "Do you need anything ironed?" when we rushed about in the morning? Who would tease me for smelling like a fruit salad when I went to bed with citrus moisturizer slathered over my entire self? All the things my husband was to me made it difficult to imagine there was someone else like him.

I was passing through the stage of darkness into vibrant light. Does God intend for me to live my remaining years alone? But how could He? He knows how I valued and enjoyed marriage—a partnership.

Older men seemed eager for a "trophy." No one interested in dating me shared my spirituality, my love of music, children, home and nature. Was there no one my age or, better yet, younger? Women should be five years older than their husbands, I have read, to ensure longer life together.

I purchased a plate for my front door with the inscription from Joshua 24:15, "As for me and my house, we will serve the Lord." I was making a statement that all who entered my home would see. Someone jokingly said, "It serves another purpose, Jan. It eliminates the riff-raff!" It eliminates only those who are uncomfortable around someone like me who is happy, loves life, loves God and wants to share that happiness.

℘

Our young female pastor is a special friend whom I adore. Pastor Laurie and I have often shared "girl talk." One day she reminded me that I, like all people, am a special child of God and that when considering a life partner, I should not be unevenly yoked. Being reminded of the Biblical concept of being joined with one who shares all the aspects of life that I hold dear became a true comfort. She said, "I know there is someone for you, Jan. I just know it!" Her expression of confidence gave me hope and excitement that day. Surely, walking and working in His kingdom would expose me to the kind of person who would see me as a potential mate. How I love Laurie for her honest friendship and love.

One thing is certain. Whether it is in a committed love relationship or marriage, I will not be unevenly yoked.

Dating

My first date after divorce was frightening. It was a personal disaster. The gentleman was a nice person, but he wasn't my husband. I felt I was betraying a covenant I made at an altar many years before. I returned home that night and sobbed and raged. "Damn you—damn you for leaving me and making me go through this!"

Dating can be hard work! Some men whom I have dated are several years older. They are near retirement and living at a slower pace. My pace is rapid. My life is exciting. I have energy I haven't had since my youth. I don't want to lose the vigor I enjoy so much.

Friends have "surprised" me with special dates that are fun, but it's interesting how their choices for me contrast with my personal wishes.

The most disappointing situations are with people who have been divorced and are afraid to enter a new, committed relationship. My first heartbreak came from nearly falling head over heels in love with someone who seemed to fit into my life beautifully.

Then there are those who assume that a divorced woman wants only a sexual involvement and will eagerly become involved with any man to serve that purpose. I have those needs as well. But life is different now, and I am determined not to lose my self-respect.

I think of how wonderful it will be to be in love, to give and receive love with that special person. Desire is a very strong emotion. Yes, I ache with desire at times. One does not easily forget the marvelous intimacies of marriage, the feelings of oneness.

If I am to find a new life partner, he will have to be one who believes as I do, who shares the love of family and young people as I do, who loves the woods and water, and much more. Surely there is someone special for me, and I pray that God, in His goodness, will bring that person to me while we're young enough to share this life with exuberance.

When an old school friend came to visit last summer, he told of his romantic courtship with his new wife. He lived with his son and she lived with her son, both in the same small community in the Pacific Northwest. He had noticed her, but couldn't determine how to introduce himself in a gentlemanly manner. When he and his son suddenly decided to take a fishing trip, he wondered what to do with the cake he just baked. "Ah-ha!" He could use the cake as an introduction. So he boldly carried the cake to her doorstep, introduced himself and explained that he had noticed that she lived with a son, just as he did. Could she, perhaps, use the rest of this cake? Evidently she was enchanted by this move, and they became friends. They eventually married to live happily ever after on a yacht in a bay on the Pacific coast.

I keep checking my doorstep...!

I often question the wisdom God used in creating men and women in such different form. Why couldn't we be of similar minds? Why does it have to be so difficult to ascertain feelings, thoughts, ideas? It's not for us to know, I'd guess. But I still wonder why women think one way and men think another. We need one thing—they need another. How are we supposed to figure all this out?

I don't have the answers. In the meantime, I will continue with my life and enjoy the blessings that come with each new day. But it would be wonderful to have a partner to share this new life.

Teen Years or Keen Years?

Some things never change! I parked the car in the garage and dashed into the house, turned on the curling iron, stripped off my clothes and dashed back across the hall to take a quick shower. I had to be at a meeting in an hour. The drive would take at least 15 minutes. *He'd be there!* I stood at the kitchen counter and ate a sandwich. On the way out the door I grabbed my notebook. It had only taken me 35 minutes, so I'd be early. Whew! I was too excited to stay home...it would add to the excitement to be there a little early, to anticipate his arrival.

On the way to the meeting it hit me. "This is the way you felt when you knew you'd see Billy!" I said aloud. Many years, with lots of changes, had passed since my first boyfriend. This was ridiculous—or was it wonderful? I felt like I was 15 again, and I loved it.

Tom Tipton, the famous gospel singer, refers to our golden years as the "KeenAge." The only difference between teenage and keenage is wisdom, according to Brother Tom. When starting over, it seems that my heart has danced with as much excitement as my younger heart. Sadly, it is capable of breaking just as easily. Although it is difficult, the keenage wisdom makes it possible to see things with stronger vision than before. It's fun, yes it's fun, to feel like a teenager again—it's a keen age!

More Therapy

Four years have passed since I was first alone. People often ask, "Is there anyone special in your life?" Others ask, "Do you plan to marry again?" My answer is in the negative, because there isn't anyone *very* special. When I entered into a new relationship, all my old insecurities rose to haunt me. I care for him but I have strange feelings at times. I'm afraid—am I afraid of connecting again? Am I afraid of rejection?

I don't know how to handle my feelings. I feel myself freeze up, and it frightens me! I think my actions portray aloofness. I'm not aloof, not intentionally. I'm scared to death! I don't want to wreck anything, but I'm afraid I'm giving him the wrong messages. Don't I believe I'm worthy? Certainly I *am* worthy. How can I allay the fears? I know I fear rejection. I'm afraid of falling in love, afraid he won't share my feelings and then I'll be back at square one. I don't want another disappointment, to fall back into the pit and have to endure the pain and grief that accompanies loss. The solution is to get rid of the fear and just take the opportunity and hope for the best. I don't know how to do that.

But now I feel I have fallen back, and it frightens me. I need to go back to therapy for a tune-up, to bring myself up to par and set me straight once again. It's disappointing.

*Thus began several weekly visits to my therapist. I had accomplished so much, he said, and surely should be ready to begin a serious relationship. "Yes," he assured me, "you **are** worthy of another chance. You have every right to follow your intuition and enter into a relationship."*

We talked about my fears. He reminded me of the work I had done to accomplish the growth he recognized. What happened to me was cruel—and it doesn't have to happen again. I didn't cause it; it just happened to me.

I shouldn't have hesitated to return for additional therapy. We are so much better off when we "tune up" from time to time, when we examine important issues, and evaluate how they affect our lives. We can study Scripture and pray, but when there is a deep fear or a feeling of inadequacy, it is vital that we treat ourselves to additional therapy to clear the problems, allowing us to continue our growth.

I'm thankful today for Christian therapists and counselors who work with us on our psyche but never hesitate to remind us that God is there with us, to take our hand and walk with us while we continue our healing and growth.

It would be much easier to stay in never-never land, to flounder, to get on and off the roller coaster of emotions. I had made a choice to work on situations that upset me, to process change and to grow accordingly.

I learned that it is necessary to walk through the pain, not around or over it. I had walked through the pain—it hurt! Skirting or ignoring the multitudes of issues I encountered would only prolong my journey from hurt to healing. I knew I had to continue, no matter what the cost. The summit was now in sight, and I gave myself no choice. I would forge ahead and try not to look back.

Does it ever end? Yes, it does. I believe that one day the sense of total confidence will come. We learn as young people that anything worth doing is worth doing well. We are worth the effort.

And I learned another still more important fact. I realized I was capable of loving again. It was a fear that had plagued me for a long time. Yes, I **could** *love again!*

It's Meant to be Shared

I miss sharing many of the special things that we shared as a couple.

I want to melt into my seat at the concert halls and just flow into the strains of wonderful music. I want to absolutely *thrill* to the voice or the instrument of an artist, with that person next to me who is equally thrilled. I recall how we loved so many of the same things, and it was terrific to know how he felt because of my own feelings of delight at wonderful music.

When the new snow falls like feathers from the evergreens, I need to share that scene with someone, to say, "Come to the window...look at this!" Walking outside on Saturday morning to smell the newness of spring requires another person—this moment is meant to be shared. When a rose blooms, adorned with a tear of moisture, it is required (isn't it ?) that one must call, "Oh, look! Come and see this!"

Then there are the unspoken messages—the appreciation of something wonderful—when a mere glance makes a statement of appreciation. The glance, returned, confirms our senses and leaves a warm glow within. Such communication cannot be accomplished "solo." To experience something wonderful, and hold it to myself and not share it, underscores ALONE.

*In the healing process, we learn that one **can** learn to live alone and be content. One **can** participate in activities as an individual. This business of learning to live and act as a single person is very good. One has to assume that an individual **must** be able to cope, to exist as a person in solitude.*

Many people prefer to remain single and live happy, fulfilled lives. We have the freedom of choice. I had a marriage proposal early in this process but chose not to accept it. I have had no regrets.

My life today is a solitary journey. I must make every effort to make it worthwhile, to be enriched by everything around me. The table has been set. It is filled with opportunities. It is up to me to make it a banquet!

Be Gentle

I need to make decisions. I need to decide whether or not I'm going to sell this house. It's so comfortable now. But it's beginning to cost me too much. I'd rather have something "less" and enjoy other things in life. I want to travel more, to see and learn more.

It is difficult to think about leaving this home. These walls have protected me against the outside world for a long time. This place reflects who I am as a person. This place has allowed the creativity in me to blossom again.

I think of my family and friends and how I've enjoyed having them here with me. David reminded me, "Where you are, that's home." I know the kids love this home because of the special times they've had here. But being together in another place would also be home, because we'd all be there together.

And then there are the memories, the days that seem vacant because this house reflects memories of events that will never occur again.

Why am I so hard on myself? What is deep within me that's so bothersome? If I'm going to abandon myself, to surrender everything every day, why am I hanging on so tightly to some of these things?

Kelsey is just a year old but has learned in her day care group to "touch gently" rather than hit or slap someone. I must remember that, to be gentle with myself.

I shouldn't create situations that will cause undue stress. The answers will unfold. I'm certain of that.

You Touched My Heart

I have met someone wonderful! Everything is so right between us. It's as if we have known each other always.

Others had warned about "games." I was certain I would recognize them. But I didn't! I *believed* his interest meant more than it did. In my naiveté, I *believed* I was being pursued.

How will I build a wall around my heart so I am not so vulnerable? It's going to be nearly impossible for me to be myself, yet pretend I don't care. I must be real. I'm not capable of anything else.

Now what do I do? Do I back away from friendship to protect myself? It has become so difficult; I'm trying so hard to keep my perspective.

One of the scariest aspects of being single is the realization that someone I believe to be a perfect match may not be interested in involvement—but simply the "thrill of the chase." It becomes like a game—a game of conquest, then fear.

The disappointment was great. I lived in a state of "if only" for months.

We feel the warmth in a glance, a touch. Why can't we address it? What within us allows us to build the walls, to wear the masks? How lovely life would be if we could be honest—if we could admit our feelings at the onset and "let them come forth" rather than stuff them, to walk backwards away from them, in fear.

Evidently I am not the only woman to have such an experience. Daphne Lewis captured my feelings in her writing called "Interweave."

Interweave

Within your eyes
lie radiant springs
of warmth and comfort's bliss.

You took my breath
and touched my heart
first blessed night we kissed.

Transgressing flesh
two spirits touched
when words failed to convey

our sacramental
bond of love
still in our hearts today.

You changed my life
you fed my soul
with your good and fruitful vine

webbed like lace
inside me,
your heart now part of mine.

© Daphne Lewis
Illuminations: An Interweave of
Thought, Identity, and Love
1992 LangMarc Publishing
San Antonio, Texas

Letting Go

Ruth, my counselor in the first months of group therapy, said it could take five years to totally recover from divorce after such a long period of marriage. "No way," I thought. "I'm going to break some kind of record and put this all behind me lots sooner." She also told me to live with so-called "blinders" on my eyes. "Don't look 'sideways' at anyone of the opposite sex for at least two years," she said, "because you're so vulnerable."

Ruth was right. It took me nearly five years to get it all together, to totally let go of the past and move ahead in complete honesty.

I knew she was right about the blinders, too. My head turned many times and I had to turn it back with force. I was swept off my feet more than once and could have jumped into a permanent relationship many times. I *was* vulnerable. I was lonely and needed to be loved and cared for. Thank God I didn't succumb. Thank God for Ruth's good advice.

How many of us know people who have walked into a new relationship with eyes wide open, only to be devastated because old "garbage" still existed and had to be dealt with in a healthy manner. Then, off into another relationship, and on and on they'd go, never to heal. How much better it is to deal with life as it's handed to us, to get on with the healing therapy and build a new and better life.

Were it not for Ruth's advice, I'd have failed in my journey back from hurt to healing. I would have connected with someone too quickly. While I still ached with pain from my circumstances, people were encouraging me to remarry. At times I felt as if I was failing myself because I didn't really want an involvement. I often wondered if something was wrong with me...if I had fears that I was hiding from myself! No, I was being protected. God, in His mercy, heard my prayer and was helping me get my life back together again.

Letting go of the past is a slow and painful process. We hang on to the familiar because it's easier that way. Separation hurts—it hurts terribly.

Moving into the fifth year made me want to celebrate! I wasn't involved with anyone and didn't care, at that point, if I was. I knew that if God had someone for me, it would be revealed to me. Besides, "they" say that when you least expect it—when you have determined it's not all that bad being alone—it's then that someone comes into your life.

I'm not going to move about in my life "pretending." Of course I am self-sufficient, but I don't want to be alone forever. Nevertheless, I'm not going to sit around and wait! Life is for the living. There's much to do. There's much to finish. There's much to begin!

It's just so good to realize I've really, actually, let go!

In My Solitude

I'm sitting in candlelight, reflecting on a perfect day. My feeling is of total contentment. So much was accomplished today!

It is a rare Saturday that I have time on my hands, when no plans have been made to share the day, or at least a part of it, with someone. Today was different. Early in the morning with my coffee cup in hand, I walked to the sun room windows and reveled in the beauty of nature surrounding me. I knew that today was going to be my very own special day.

I sorted through my collection of recordings and chose the day's background music. I reached for the boxes of photographs from the closet shelf. I submerged myself in recent photographs of trips and events, warmed by the nostalgia each one carried. Then, as the music of Grieg filled the house, I remembered the sweater I've been working on for months. As I picked up my knitting, I remembered the day I purchased the yarn in Bergen, Norway. I remembered how my cousin and I laughed and dashed from shop to shop in the rain. I smiled, warmed by the memories of those special days with loved ones.

I telephoned my mother, as I do each Saturday. As I listened to her describe a flurry of activity, I realized that I could follow a family pattern and live at least thirty more productive years. It was food for thought, something to ponder today and other days. I wondered what I will do with the rest of my life.

I prepared lunch and ate it while reading my mail. Watching the cardinals and jays at the bird feeder, I decided to spend some time outside. My cross-country skis were still in the car from last night's outing, so I drove to a nearby park and skied for a couple of hours, basking in the beauty surrounding me. I felt privileged to be alone communing with nature—content to appreciate the simple wonders of this life.

I spent the rest of the day reading, listening to music and delighting in my contentment. Now I sit in candlelight, so relaxed that I feel like I'm living in paradise.

A day in solitude is one of the most productive days I can spend. It is living proof of my ability to enjoy being alone. It provides a welcome balance, a contrast to the days filled with activity from morning to late evening. As I notice my reflection in the mirror, I see a contented Me. This person in the mirror is not the same person that lived here a few years ago.

My solitude is comfortable and warm. I feel whole. I am reminded that I am an individual, capable of caring for myself and capable of enjoying my own company. It feels good. I am renewed! It is another victory.

Forsaking All Others

I really hope I will be able to remarry, that someone will find me to be the answer to his dreams. I know I will be a good wife. An old song says, "Love is better…the second time around." Perhaps. If that is so, it's probably because it's so welcome.

For richer and poorer. Money and "things" will not be my requisite for a marriage partner. The important facet will be love and trust, the enjoyment of similar interests, a similar faith level—and just a good considerate man. Marrying for love is the only marriage. I can't imagine being married to a rich man I did not love. My life is rich right now, and it has nothing to do with money.

In sickness and in health. True love is essential with the possibilities of ill health we all face. Age is not a guide. Drastic illness comes to all ages. A loving partner will stand by, firmly, through sickness. And a loving partner will enjoy us in good times even more, with the knowledge that we are faithful—always there—in good times and in bad.

To love and to cherish. To be loved and give love with unabashed joy is ideal. I observe the warmth some couples have towards each other; their concern, their gentle friendship. They cherish and respect each other as individuals. Love is a beautiful experience.

Until death parts us. Mother confided to me recently that Dad told her, "If you go first, I want to go right away." Certainly that possibility is real, and it is a concern to the elderly. On the other hand, my contemporary, whose husband has suffered a hearing loss for many years, told me the same thing. When we have walked together for years, it is almost impossible to think of walking alone. Certainly I can relate to those feelings; I can well imagine how it feels to walk alone after death makes a visit.

Partnership, whether in marriage or business, is based on trust. Without trust, a partnership, as in any relationship, finds itself on shaky ground. I dream of a relationship in harmony, one where commitment is a pleasure and the harmony of love brings sheer joy.

Day Dreams

I'm dreaming today of where I've been and where I am today. It's a wonderful Saturday. It's probably the last warm day of fall in Minnesota. I've washed windows, done all the cleaning necessary on the inside, worked in the flower beds, shopped for groceries, and now find myself relaxing. I don't even want to turn on the radio. I'm dreamy. It's relaxing. It is good.

Sometimes when I think back on last fall, and the falls before, it seems as though I'm recalling someone else. I really have come a long way. When I recall pain, I hardly remember how it was. It's like the vacation pictures my friend Gloria talks about—by the time you have the photographs printed, you've lost the magic of the time away!

No matter. I love to daydream—to remember, and to plan ahead. But then I don't do much planning ahead. Why bother? God will handle it all just fine. I love this time of year.

We are so fortunate when we can dream. It costs nothing, and it allows us to escape for a while from the reality of a world that causes more concern than delight. It also provides a vehicle—a means of transporting ourselves from this world to a fantasy world—and likely establishes the pattern for the new and better life.

There Are No Guarantees

When I reflect upon all the great things that have happened in my life during the past few years, I'm amazed. Why is God allowing this to happen to me? It's not that I'm so good. Others are very, very good and bad things happen to them, things that try their patience and their faith.

I remember walking through the skyway one noon hour last summer, feeling as if I had the world by the tail. I felt so good at that moment, it was almost scary. How could life be nicer than this?

Two hours later I ran down that same skyway towards the parking lot, so thankful I had driven my car to work. Dad had been in an automobile accident, and I was racing the clock to get to St. Mary's Hospital in Duluth. I was scared to death. As I moved along so quickly, I couldn't help recalling my feelings of elation a short time before.

I drove to Duluth in record time. Strangely, I didn't think about what might lay ahead. Before I left, I prayed for calm. I drove the entire two and one-half hours without concern. It was like I was in a bubble all the way. I was being guided carefully. Dad's condition stabilized; he was discharged from the hospital after a few days. I was able to stay with my parents to help them adjust to a period of recovery.

We know that, as Christians, we are not immune from trouble. We are, however, given the strength and peace of God's grace which provides hope and comfort.

Life Moves On

Time moved fast—too fast at times. Activities filled my calendar and left me little time for myself. The days that had once been empty were now full to over-flowing. Now the "alone" times were coveted. I loved the solitude and used it for special projects, combined with welcome meditation or quiet time. These times of reflection made me thankfully aware of the amazing healing that had occurred in my life.

In the process of change, it became clear that God intended to use me in His ministry. One after another, He has opened doors to new and varied opportunities to share the Good News of Christ with others. He is holding me to my promise, "If you help me, I'll help others."

Life is nice. Life is good. I'm so content with life as it flows today. I'm busy with commitments, yet I have lots of free time for myself. It's balanced and it's fulfilling. I feel good about me, about where I'm going and how life is unfolding.

It seems that finally, after such a long time, I have found a peace—a contentment—that feels good. Now I can simply "be who I am!"

I feel like a "normal" person, whatever that is. Dare I say that I've "arrived?" Sure...say it! "I think I have arrived!!"

Christmas Is Coming

I'm excited! I love Christmas! I love the warm glow of candlelight, Christmas music playing softly in the background, the fragrances of almond and pine. This is Christmas, 1992, the first Christmas I have felt like a whole person since that fateful day nearly six years ago. Christmas is one huge reason I worked so hard to rebuild my life. No one should have to live with tarnished memories at this wonderful time of the year.

Kathy called last night. She and Pat are going to Chicago for Christmas. It's a rare opportunity to see most of Pat's family, and his mom will celebrate her 70th birthday. They'll all enjoy seeing Kelsey, who is just learning to walk. Kathy seemed apologetic! I reminded her that the other kids and their families will be here with me—that all of my children have spouses from wonderful, large families, and we have to share holidays. I was touched by her sensitivity, her constant warmth.

My life has come full circle, and I'm back to celebrating, entertaining and loving Christmas. I am so truly thankful. Christmas may always be different each year, but it's okay. In addition to my growing family, I have wonderful friends. I need space and time for them. Foremost, I need to reflect on the true meaning—the *real* gift of Christmas.

Christmas is the time to share the blessings we have been so freely given. I attended candlelight services late on Christmas Eve with a friend who was also alone.

Christmas Day dawned with bright sunshine. It didn't seem right to be alone Christmas morning, so I invited my friend Marty to come over early in the morning, "...and come in your robe!" We exchanged gifts, had coffee and traditional Christmas foods, and just laughed at ourselves about how fun—how very special—this morning was.

My family arrived later that morning, and we had a beautiful time of celebration that lasted nearly three days. As I looked at each of them that day, I said a silent prayer of thanksgiving. I had conquered the agony of "tomorrow" (the fateful day after Christmas) and celebrated a victory that I alone could appreciate.

I have been given the greatest gifts! I have the gifts of love, peace, joy, happiness. I have the gifts of the Holy Spirit! God has blessed me so richly. I cherish each gift and vow to use them, each to the utmost of my ability.

"...what manner can I borrow to thank thee, Dearest Friend."

My Cup Runneth Over

I'll be so glad when 1992 is over. It's been a good year in so many ways, but I'm glad anyway. Lots of good things have happened, but there's been pain too. Pain of separation (even though I want to separate) from situations. It has been difficult to separate from the singles group at church, but it's time. I no longer feel "single" but feel whole as an individual. I want to be associated with others, other organizations, couples—just people in general. And I am enjoying my work with the youth at church more than ever.

I feel as if I'm graduating from someplace special today, on this eve of a new year. I remember someone joking about having a Ph.D. from the School of Hard Knocks. That's my most important degree. I have a doctorate in surviving!

There was a communion service at church this New Year's Eve. The chapel was dimly lit and Christmas music was playing softly on the sound system. Two teams of two people each were in the chancel ready to pray with individuals or couples and to give them communion.

I walked up to the chancel towards Pastor Tedd and his prayer partner. Tedd took both my hands and said, "Lindsey (his daughter) was here and prayed a prayer of thanksgiving that she had bonded with the youth group. It means so much to her." Then he said, "These are the fruits of your ministry, Jan."

Good thing I had stuffed a tissue in my sleeve, because I used it! His words amazed me and thrilled me. My feelings at that moment were of great appreciation. Youth ministry had blessed my life profoundly. Tedd asked me if I wanted to pray about anything special, so he and his partner each took one of my hands as I knelt to pray. I prayed aloud that God would guide me in the ministries provided to me, that I would be worthy of all the blessings that have been given to me. Then, suddenly, the words just came out of my mouth without warning. "And God, please God, bring me someone to share this life. Bring me a partner to share this good life, someone who will work with me to your glory." Well, wasn't that interesting! It seemed that right there, while kneeling at the communion rail, words articulating my deep-seated desire had spilled right out of my mouth.

The woman prayed and asked that my prayers be honored. Then Tedd prayed and thanked God for me, mentioned my "joyful spirit," for my work at the church. He said, "God, I don't know how you go about doing this, but stir up the heart of someone special for Jan." I felt embarrassed at first, but then thought, "Why not?" God made me who I am. He made me a loving person, one who is honest and sharing. He knows me better than anyone. He wasn't surprised at that prayer, I'm sure.

As they prepared to serve communion to me, Tedd asked, "Would you like to be anointed?" I said, "Yes, I would."

Tedd then made the sign of the cross upon my forehead with oil, the first time that had been done for me. I felt like I was being ordained. I guess I was, in a way. I felt the love of God was being "sealed" within me so I could step into the new year in total renewal.

As I walked back to my seat I had to sit there for a few minutes to pull myself together. It was like a benediction of all that had transpired in the past year. My feelings are difficult to describe, but emotion welled up within me and kept growing. I had felt "full" before, but this emotion was overflowing! It felt like this had been the funeral for the Jan who had often been in pain, not only in the past year but during all the years before this day. It became the resurrection service for my new life!

I walked down the long hallway to the north parking lot. As I got closer to the door, I burst into tears. I held myself together as best I could until I got into the car, locked the door, and then wept tears of happiness. I thanked God for people whom I named, for places and things. I thanked Him especially for my spirit, that it was so noticeable that Tedd called it joyful. That spirit had been dulled for such a long time. I had been renewed—so totally renewed. What a gift! What a wonderful gift for the New Year!

I went home and sat by the light of the Christmas tree and basked in these good feelings. I went to bed at 11:00 p.m., so anxious for tomorrow, to begin a New Year!

It's over. All the trial and tribulations, all the new experiences that were difficult and painful, all the "trying," the "faking it," the measured steps to get beyond the uncomfortable feelings I harbored. It was all over.

This was a new beginning. Today is the First Day of the Rest of My Life! Now I am equipped for anything. Now I can face anything, and in better form than ever before. Now I'm just me, a simple person, who holds the key to life. God said He'd take all that pain, all those awful days from me forever, and He did! He provided me with the same "owner's manual" He gave everyone—His word through the Scriptures. Now it's up to me. My God, it feels so good!

He anointed my head with oil.

My cup runneth over.

The Summit!

Well, I made it! Today I'm at the mountaintop! I feel whole again and it feels good! In the process of living life, I know I will slide on the rocks and slip on the path. I know I will feel lonely at times, but I know I am not alone in this life. I have learned how to abandon the concerns, to dwell on the mountain "highs" rather than in the valley "lows." The old heartbreak and pain have been set aside for better things. The fulfillment I have today is greater than I ever dreamed possible.

As I have prepared the reflections for this journal, I have been amazed and delighted to see how God used individuals—special people—as stepping stones in my journey from hurt to healing. We never know when we, our words or our actions, will be used in someone's life to alter the course, to enhance another's pathway.

I reach the summit in solemnity, stricken with the reality of the awesome God we worship.

A recent retreat weekend with the church youth group became still another step on my journey. I was touched with the reality of God's love as evidenced through these young people and their love for me. The theme song for the event was taken from Psalm 51.

> *Create in me a clean heart, O God*
> *And renew a right spirit within me.*
> *Cast me not away from thy presence, O Lord*
> *And take not thy Holy Spirit from me!*
> *Restore unto me the joy of thy salvation*
> *And renew a right spirit within me.*
> *Create in me a clean heart, O God!*

As we sang this song, accompanied by mellow guitars, I felt overwhelmed with the magnitude of God's work in and through me during the past few years. As we exchanged warm glances through tear-filled eyes, I was thrilled with the majesty of the moment. My tears were mixed. There were tears of joy at my renewal. There were tears of sadness that some of these young-sters, so innocent and content today, would also encoun-ter immeasurable pain in their lives. Then there were my happy tears of thanksgiving that we have a God who loves us enough to walk with us, to carry us when the burden is greatest, to free us and make us whole.

It is exciting to realize how God has worked in and through me! I am not unique. It is a simple fact that I had to change my situation, to become accustomed to a new and different way of life. Asking Him to carry my burden was my personal key to victory. There is no way I could have healed myself.

I made a promise to help others who are faced with the pain of separation find a new life. It is my fervent prayer that your life will be made easier, your pathway smoother, by reading this—my personal journal of ex-periences *when I was first alone.*

Index of Vignettes

Part 1—Through Shadowed Valleys

He is Gone 3
Who Will Help Me? 5
David 7
The Ghosts of Christmases Past 8
Our Bedroom 9
Sleep 10
Dreams 12
The Neighbors 13
Abandoned 15
What Can They Say? 17
Longing 19
Pain 20
Church 21
I Can't Read! 23
The Work Place 24
My Children 25
Romans 8:28 27
Stress 28

Part 2—Beside Still Waters

Therapy 33
Familiar Scenes 35
Couples 36
Summer 37
Going to the Well 39
Dependency 41
You Can Do It, Sister 43
Safety 45
The Search for "Me" 46
Lisa 48
Twelve Steps to Healing 50
Abandonment—The Prayer 52
The Prayer of Abandonment 53
Why Did You Leave? 54
Divorce Granted 58

It's All in a Name 60
From This Day Forward 61
Questions 63
Running Away 64
What is Lost 65
What About Me? 67

Part 3—On Mountain Paths

On My Knees 71
Friends are Friends...Forever 74
Used as an Angel 76
Release on the Mountaintop 77
Singles—A New Ministry 80
Forgiveness 82
We're Single Again 84
Laughter 85
Heavenly Sunshine 86
The Awakening 87
Conflicting Feelings 89
On Being Religious 91
I Don't Want to Go! 93
What's Going On?! 94
The Boot Strap Syndrome 95
Rebuilding 97
Don't Be Unevenly Yoked 98
Dating 100
Teen Years or Keen Years? 102
More Therapy 103
It's Meant to be Shared 105
Be Gentle 107
You Touched My Heart 108
Letting Go 110
In My Solitude 112
Forsaking All Others 114
Day Dreams 116
There Are No Guarantees 117
Life Moves On 118
Christmas Is Coming 119
My Cup Runneth Over 121
The Summit! 124

To Order Copies

☎ **Telephone Orders:** Call 1-800-864-1648

✉ **Postal Orders:** LangMarc Publishing, PO Box 33817, San Antonio, Texas 78265-3817. USA.

When I Was First Alone
hard cover $12.95

Quantity Discounts: 10% discount for 3-4 copies, 15% for 5-9 copies, 20% for 10 or more copies.

Shipping: UPS or Priority Mail: $3 for 1 or 2 books, 50¢ each additional book.

Book Rate: $1.50 for the first book and 50¢ each additional book. (Delivery up to three weeks)

Sales Tax: Texas residents only, add 7.25% (94¢ per book).

Send a Gift to a Friend: We will mail directly. Shipping cost to each address will be $3.00 UPS or $1.50 book rate.

Please send payment with order.

Books Cost: _____

Shipping: _____

Check Enclosed: _____

Name and Address for order delivery:

_____

_____

_____

_____